Never Far Away

# Never Far Away

The Auschwitz Chronicles of Anna Heilman

Edited by
Sheldon Schwartz

Introduction by Dieter K. Buse and Juergen C. Doerr

Afterword by Joel Prager

UNIVERSITY OF
CALGARY
PRESS

University of Calgary Press
2500 University Drive NW
Calgary, Alberta
Canada  T2N 1N4

**National Library of Canada Cataloguing in Publication Data**

Heilman, Anna, 1928-
Never far away

    Includes bibliographical references and index.
      ISBN 1-55238-040-8

  1. Heilman, Anna, 1928-  2. Auschwitz (Concentration camp)
3.  Holocaust, Jewish (1939-1945)—Personal narratives.
4. Jews—Poland—Biography.  I. Schwartz, Sheldon.  II. Title.
DS135.P63H44 2001    940.53'18'092      C2001-911197-5

Canadä We acknowledge the financial support of the Government of Canada through the Book Publishing Industry Development Program (BPIDIP) for our publishing activities.

The Canada Council for the Arts
Le Conseil des Arts du Canada

Printed and bound in Canada by AGMV Marquis.
Cover design by Kristina Schuring.

∞ This book is printed on acid-free paper.

# Contents

To Marta, who saved my life,
and
to Sheldon, who saved my story.

# Foreword

This book consists of the diaries and memoirs of Anna Heilman, written over the half century between 1944 and 1994.

I learned of my mother-in-law's diaries while preparing an information booklet for a memorial ceremony in 1991 at Yad Vashem, the museum and memorial to the victims of the Holocaust located in Jerusalem. The ceremony was held to dedicate a sculpture to the memory of four young women: Esther (Estusia) Wajcblum (Anna Heilman's sister), Regina Safirztajn, Ala Gertner, and Roza Robota. These women were executed in January 1945 for their part in the October 1944 uprising at Auschwitz.

After the ceremony, I asked Anna to translate the diaries that she wrote in Polish between 1944 and 1945. This material, originally written in Auschwitz and Belgium, includes the chapters entitled "The Warsaw Ghetto" and "Auschwitz" and the two sections in "The October 1944 Uprising," chapter entitled "Premonition" and "Eustasia's Last Letter." The original diaries are with Anna Heilman.

I also asked Anna to write supplementary material to provide context and continuity. This includes most of the explanatory footnotes and the chapters "Warsaw: Before World War II"; "Majdanek" (except for the section "In Majdanek," which was written in 1975); the "October 1944 Uprising" (other than the two sections, "Premonition" and "Estusia's Last Letter," noted above); and "The Ghost of the Past is Never Far Away." This material was written by Anna between 1991 and 1994.

As English is not Anna's first language, I edited the manuscript for grammar, while striving to preserve the authenticity of Anna's literary voice, which ranges from that of a fifteen-year-old child to that of a woman in her sixties. I also ordered the material to provide a logical flow for the reader.

Many people have helped to make the publication of this book possible. I would like to thank Anna Feldman, Alvin Finkel of Athabasca University, Georgina Taylor of the Saskatchewan Indian Federated College, Walter Hildebrandt and John King of the University of Calgary, Juergen C. Doerr of St. Thomas University, Dieter K. Buse of Laurentian University, Michael Marrus of the University of Toronto, Joel Prager, and Noa Schwartz. Most of all, I would like to thank Anna Heilman for the honour of knowing her and for the privilege of working with her.

*Sheldon Schwartz*

# Introduction

## by Dieter K. Buse and Juergen C. Doerr

During World War II, millions of Jews and other victims of Nazi racial policy entered a valley of death; only a small minority emerged at the other end.[1] Anna Heilman (née Wajcblum) was one of the lucky ones. Her memoir/diary of her passage through that valley is graphic, lucid, and moving. This is the story of a young woman born into a middle-class Jewish family in Warsaw. She relates her happy childhood; the sudden awareness of the danger of an aggressive Germany; the Nazi attack on Warsaw and the occupation of that city; the Warsaw ghetto; the deportation of her family to the Majdanek death camp; separation from her parents and her subsequent transfer to the Auschwitz death camp; her life and her sister's life in the camp and in the nearby Birkenau work factory; the hanging of her sister for sabotage, that is, resistance activities; the evacuation from Auschwitz in January 1945; and finally, the death march to Neustadt-Glewe (in Mecklenburg), where the survivors were turned over to the Americans and from where she was taken to Belgium.

For readers familiar with the events of the Holocaust, the following explanatory notes may serve as a review. For others, these notes will place the major issues related in Anna Heilman's narrative in context and provide background on the Holocaust, consider the nature of memoirs, and offer a few suggestions for further reading.

---

1 For a general overview of the Holocaust, readers might consult the entry "Holocaust," by Michael Marrus, in Dieter K. Buse and Juergen C. Doerr, eds., *Modern Germany: An Encyclopedia of History, People, and Culture, 1871–1990* (New York: Garland, 1998). The cross-references at the end of the entry lead to related topics relevant to these memoirs. For further reading, see Donald L. Niewyk, ed., *The Holocaust: Problems and Perspectives of Interpretation* (Boston: Houghton Mifflin, 1997).

## Jews and Poles to 1939

The relationship between Jews and Poles defies comfortable generalization: each community displayed considerable diversity. The religious, cultural, social, and political complexity of Poland's Jewish community paralleled the even greater variety of the multi-ethnic – Byelorussian, Lithuanian, German, Russian, Ukrainian – and multi-religious – Uniate, Protestant, Muslim, Orthodox, Catholic – composition of Polish society in general.

To oversimplify, Polish Jews at the beginning of the twentieth century could be divided into three primary categories: (1) those who sought to maintain both their ethnic identity and their religion, (2) those who retained their Jewish identity but not their religion, and (3) those who were fully assimilated and had ended their affiliation with Jewry. The Wajcblum family appears to have been in transition from the second to the third category during the 1930s. Nearly all Polish Jews were affected by the strains of the modernization process, by increases in population, by continuing poverty, and by the rising intensity of nationalism, especially Polish nationalism and Zionism.

It must be recalled that pre-World War I Poland was a politically partitioned community. Late in the eighteenth century, Poland had lost its independence and had been divided among Austria, Prussia, and Russia. Foreign rule and the desire for independence exacerbated tensions among the competing national groups within the larger Polish community.

World War I intensified the problems of Poland's Jews. As a separate community with no particular affiliation with the competing military and political powers, Polish Jews were criticized for not committing themselves to one side or the other; they were also physically caught between the combatant forces. At the end of the Great War, a number of Jews gave their support to the newly established and independent Polish Republic, and some volunteered to serve in the forces of Marshall Pilsudski, the dominant political figure of the young republic.

The new Poland could not escape the European-wide economic disruption, the heightened ethnic animosities, and the political radicalism of the inter-war period. Certainly the Jews of Poland (some 2 million in 1921; 3.35 million by 1939) faced their share of difficulties. Though some, like the Wajcblums, enjoyed all of the attributes – holidays on the sea coast, nannies, trips – of middle-class existence, many Polish Jews lived in poverty and squalor. Both Polish state officials and the burgeoning Polish middle class sought to push traditional Jewish traders to the sidelines. As in Germany, resentment grew over the prominence of Jews in national, professional, and intellectual life.

Scholars and other commentators have debated the condition of Jews in Poland before 1939. Some have viewed the situation as a prelude to the Holocaust; others, while recognizing the problems faced by Jews, have concluded that other minorities, such as the Ukrainians and the Byelorussians, were worse off.

If, for example, we choose three experts on Poland, the British historian Norman Davies, the Israeli scholar Yisrael Gutman, and the American authority William Hagen, we find some noteworthy differences of opinion on the nature and significance of Polish–Jewish relations and, in particular, on anti-Semitism in Poland in the inter-war decades.[2] To some extent, their varying assessments reflect different emphases. Davies analyzes the conditions of Jews in Poland as part of his magisterial study of the history of Poland. Gutman, who has published extensively on the fate of Poland's Jews during the Holocaust, examines the relations between the two peoples more from the Jewish than the Polish perspective. Hagen explores the commonalities of central and eastern European anti-Semitism of the 1930s.

These authors agree that anti-Semitism was noticeable in Polish society; for centuries, it had been a noteworthy feature of Polish–Jewish relations. The post-1918 multi-ethnic Polish Republic did not treat all its citizens with an even hand. Unassimilated Jews, in general, did not have access to employment in the civil service and to related positions in the military, the schools, and the railways. Their acceptance into the professions was not to exceed their proportion of the population. Jewish schools were not subsidized by the state, though they were allowed. Economically and socially, the condition of most Jews declined in the 1930s. The Jewish population increased significantly from 2.7 million in 1931 to 3.35 million by 1939. Four hundred thousand emigrated; many more would have gone to Palestine or to the United States had the opportunity been present. The modernization of Polish society – industrial expansion, the growth of the Polish middle class and of peasant cooperatives – hurt traditional Jewish small business.

---

2 Norman Davies, *God's Playground: A History of Poland in Two Volumes*. Vol. 2, *1795 to the Present* (New York: Columbia University Press, 1982); Yisrael Gutman, Ezra Mendelsohn, Jehuda Reinharz, and Chone Shmeruk, eds., *The Jews of Poland between Two World Wars* (Hanover, NH: University Press of New England, 1989). In the latter work, see especially Emanuel Melzer, "Antisemitism in the Last Years of the Second Republic"; and William Hagen, "Before the 'Final Solution': Toward a Comparative Analysis of Political Antisemitism in Interwar Germany and Poland," *Journal of Modern History* 68 (June 1996): 351–81.

At the same time, the racial discriminations suffered by Jews were not exceptional, at least in the opinion of Davies.[3] He asserts that other nationalities were also victimized – probably more so – while Jews in some of the states neighbouring Poland were subject to greater anti-Jewish hysteria and violence. Of the major political parties, only one, the National Democrats, agitated against "the native foreigners in our midst," but, according to Davies, their nativism was directed against all non-Poles, including Germans and Ukrainians.[4] Gutman and Hagen assess the situation differently. The former points out that Jews were treated unlike other minorities: Ukrainians and Byelorussians were mistreated, but their right to reside on Polish land was not questioned,[5] whereas not all segments of Polish society accorded Jews this right.

Both Gutman and Hagen demonstrate the anti-Semitic thrust of the radical-right National Democratic Party, Poland's equivalent of the National Socialists. Hagen notes the explicitly anti-Semitic policies of the post-Pilsudski government, which in his view "bore strong resemblances to prewar Nazi practices,"[6] and of the government-sponsored coalition of the centre, the Camp of National Unity (OZON). For example, in 1939, OZON backbenchers drafted legislation similar to the Nazi exclusionary Nuremberg Laws.[7]

In contrast to Gutman and Davies, Hagen does not identify Polish anti-Semitism with the Nazi version, though he nevertheless stresses significant similarities between the two.

Davies asserts that the various anti-Semitic groupings had little influence, that their agitation was countered by the authorities, and that leftist political parties and the intelligentsia tended to be pro-Jewish. Davies' more positive assessment of pre-war Polish–Jewish relations finds that Jews were comparatively well integrated into the larger Polish community. Jewish culture – literature, music, theatre, film – flourished, as did the Jewish press and Jewish political groupings. Jewish social organizations such as hospitals, orphanages, sports clubs, musical societies, and cooperatives expanded.

---

3  Davies, 261.

4  Ibid.

5  Yisrael Gutman, "Polish Antisemitism between the Wars: An Overview," in Gutman et al.

6  Hagen, 361.

7  See also Melzer.

The confidence and joy of life evident in Anna Heilman's account of her family may have been typical of the Jewish middle classes in inter-war Poland, but it was a life not all Jews experienced. Within the broader contextual framework, individual experiences chart their own way.

The record on the condition of the Republic's Jews is thus at best ambiguous; there were good reasons for concern. In explaining Polish anti-Semitism, Gutman notes the absence of any significant "aggressive political action with genocidal overtones." Yet he also notes that

> popular anti-Semitism ... when combined with the objective conditions prevailing in interwar Poland (such as the sheer number of Jews, their economic plight and so forth) and with the outside influences, particularly the rapprochement with Nazi Germany [in 1934/35] and the inspiration it provided, turned Polish anti-Semitism into a combustible mixture in the late 1930s.[8]

Davies asserts, "The destruction of Polish Jewry during the Second World War ... was in no way connected to their earlier tribulations."[9] The cause of the destruction lay in Nazi Germany's expansionist and racist policies. Regardless of the experts' differences about the nature of anti-Semitism in inter-war Poland, only 369,000, or eleven percent of Poland's pre-war Jewish population survived the Final Solution.

Hitler's war made possible the destruction of the majority of Europe's Jews. Most of the death camps were set up by the Nazis in Poland. However, the Poles were also the victims of Nazi racist policies. Their elites were subject to eliminationist policies, although certainly not to the same extent as the Jews. Under these conditions of unimaginable duress, to what extent did the two peoples support each other? Again, the assessments of the historians vary. Whereas Davies notes the suffering of both Poles and Jews at the hands of the Germans and the aid at times given to Jews by their compatriots, Gutman details the further intensification of Polish anti-Semitism.[10] For example, he is critical of the lack of interest in the fate of the Jews on the part of the Polish government-in-exile in London and of the Polish Underground, and of the latter's failure to hinder the destruction of Poland's Jews.

---

8  Gutman, 107.

9  Davies, 263.

10  See, for example, Gutman's essays in Michael Marrus, ed., *Public Opinion and Relations to the Jews in Nazi Europe*. Vol. 1, pt. 5 of *The Nazi Holocaust. Historical Articles on the Destruction of European Jews* (Westport, CT: Meckler, 1989).

## The Warsaw Ghetto

On September 1, 1939, German forces invaded Poland and quickly defeated the Polish forces. By November, the invaders had reached the walls of Warsaw. Twenty days later, the city surrendered. The defeated country was divided into three parts, with the eastern area taken over by the Soviet Union and northwestern Poland annexed into the quickly expanding Reich. The south and central part, designated as the General Gouvernement, came under German occupation directed by Governor-General Hans Frank.

Warsaw was the primary but certainly not the exclusive focus of Nazi anti-Jewish policies. Not only was the city the Polish capital, it had come to play a central role for the Jews of Poland and even Jewry throughout the world. In 1914, Jews made up 38 percent of Warsaw's population. That percentage had declined to 29.1 by 1939 (375,000 out of a total population of 1,289,000). While the Warsaw community lacked the deep historical roots and traditions of other Jewish centres in Poland, it demonstrated the active role of Jews in modern Polish life.

True to the rabid anti-Semitic ideology of the Nazi state, the occupiers introduced into the General Gouvernement area a steady stream of policies regulating Jewish life. Jews, for example, were forced to wear on their outer clothing a white ribbon with a blue Star of David; were barred from the professions, restaurants, and public parks; and were subjected to a curfew. The goal was progressively to segregate and isolate the Jews of Poland. Not only were the Jews to be publicly humiliated and contained within their quarters, they were oppressed economically through dismissal from their jobs, the denial of pensions or other social welfare measures, plain robbery by the occupiers, and confiscation of savings and cash. In ever larger numbers, they were conscripted to work for the Nazis, while their isolation from the non-Jewish community was intensified, primarily by moving urban Jews into ghettos.

By November 16, 1940, the Warsaw ghetto was sealed.[11] Within the ghetto, conditions steadily deteriorated. A year later, more than 450,000 Jews had been squeezed into the confined area: 108,000 per square kilometre. Food and heating supplies were totally inadequate. In 1941,

---

11 On the Warsaw ghetto, see, for example, Yisrael Gutman, *The Jews of Warsaw, 1939–1943: Ghetto, Underground, Revolt* (Bloomington, IN: Indiana University Press, 1982) and Israel Gutman, *Resistance: The Warsaw Ghetto Uprising* (Boston: Houghton Mifflin, 1994).

for example, some 43,000 died. To facilitate the governance – and exploitation – of the Warsaw ghetto that they had forcibly created, the German authorities, at the initiative of Reinhard Heydrich, head of the German security police and second most powerful man in the SS, decreed the creation of a council of Jewish elders, the *Judenrat*. It was to act as intermediary between the occupiers and the ghettoized Jews of Warsaw: a control agency disguised as a form of self-governance. The hopeless task the council faced was to protect fellow Jews from conquerors determined to eliminate the Jews from Europe.

The responsibilities of the *Judenrat* within the ghetto included the essentials for survival: food, housing, public health, but also justice, including police and jails. A large bureaucracy – more than 2,000 employees – was created. Given the desperate conditions within the ghetto and the lack of training of the officials, it is not surprising that corruption within this rudimentary civil service was rampant. One of the most difficult tasks was to provide the German authorities with labourers forced to work under steadily worsening conditions. By the summer of 1940, many Jews were sent to labour camps. Considering the harsh conditions imposed on them, the inhabitants of the ghetto displayed amazing ingenuity in mastering the arts of survival, much of it guided by a plethora of self-help groups and organizations that came into being alongside the official *Judenrat*. Political parties and youth groups continued to function and to engage in various underground activities. Anna Heilman herself recorded her participation in some of the youth groups and her consequent discovery of her Jewishness.

In July 1942, mass deportations from the ghetto began and continued to September 12. Within a seven-week period, about 300,000 Jews were taken from the ghetto, the vast majority (265,000) to the newly completed Treblinka death camp, where they were summarily killed. Approximately 10,000 were murdered in Warsaw during the deportation process, and 11,580 were transported to forced labour camps. About 8,000 managed to escape. By the end of September 1942, approximately 50,000 to 60,000 were left in the Warsaw ghetto, mostly men who could be used for labour.[12] Anna and her family were among the remnants of the once-flourishing Warsaw Jewish community. They – at least Anna and her sister Estusia – thus experienced the uprising of the ghetto's inhabitants against their Nazi oppressors. Sporadic resistance was precipitated by the expulsions of the

---

12  Gutman, *Resistance*, 133.

summer of 1942; its achievements were, however, minimal. But during the fall, a Jewish Fighting Force was created. It became active as the Germans, on January 18, 1943, began their second major expulsion from the ghetto. A brief battle ensued: the ghetto's inhabitants were no longer willing to accept their fate passively. In April, Jewish insurgents launched a well-prepared uprising against the powerful German military forces. Only a month later was the resistance subdued.

Anna and her family were among the last of the Warsaw Jews to be forcefully removed. They were shipped to the Majdanek death camp just outside the Lublin city limits. It was as vicious as any of the others. Of the estimated 200,000 killed within its walls, 125,000 were Jews. Upon arrival, the two Wajcblum girls were separated from their parents; they would never see them again. In August, Anna and Estusia were sent to the Auschwitz death camp.

## Auschwitz

Auschwitz, more than any other geographical place, connotes the horrors and enormity of the crime designated as the Holocaust.[13] It was the largest of the concentration camps constructed by the Nazis; its conditions were the most severe. In its death camp at nearby Birkenau (Auschwitz II), approximately 1.1 million Jews were murdered between March 1942 and November 1944. In addition, approximately 210,000 non-Jews (Poles, gypsies, Soviet prisoners of war, and others) were deported to the camp during its operation. Auschwitz was the centrepiece of the Nazi effort to eliminate the Jews from Europe, the centrepiece of the "Final Solution" machinery that ultimately murdered close to six million of Europe's eleven million Jews.

The town of Auschwitz (Oświêcim, in Polish) is located about fifty kilometres from Krakow and 286 from Warsaw. Since the partition of Poland in the late eighteenth century, Auschwitz had been part of the Hapsburg Empire. When the Germans defeated the Poles in 1939, the town of about 12,000 inhabitants was incorporated into the expanded Reich. In 1940, SS officials decided to construct a concentration camp in

---

13 See, for example, Debórah Dwork and Robert Jan van Pelt, *Auschwitz. 1270 to the Present* (New York: W.W. Norton, 1996), and Yisrael Gutman and Michael Berenbaum, eds., *Anatomy of the Auschwitz Death Camp* (Bloomington, IN: Indiana University Press, 1994).

the generally climatically inhospitable location. The purpose and nature of the camp evolved over a period of time from a holding area for Polish prisoners to a huge complex of units including industrial sites employing forced labour for the German war machine and the killing machinery that systematically liquidated over one million Jews from 1942 to 1945. Auschwitz thus became a complex of camps. A number of industrial plants, owned by such firms such as Siemens-Schuckert, IG Farbenindustrie, and Weichsel Union Metallwerke, operated in association with Krupp, were constructed in the area to take advantage of the thousands of forced labourers. Worker prisoners were also used in mines and in agriculture. A women's camp was set up in March 1942. It was subsequently moved to Birkenau, where by January 1944 it held over 27,000 prisoners. Anna Heilman was saved from certain death by being chosen to work in the Weichsel Union plant.

Conditions at Auschwitz were subhuman; life was at all times precarious, often depending upon the whim of some guard or overseer. The camp held some 70,000 remaining prisoners in January 1945, shortly before its evacuation just ahead of the advancing Red Army. Anna possessed the amazing strength, courage, and will to complete the death march to Neustadt-Glewe. On May 2, 1945, she successfully traversed the valley of death when the prisoners were liberated by the Russians.

**The Holocaust: Understanding the Incomprehensible**

In a university history course, students were asked how they would introduce the memoirs or the diary of a Holocaust survivor. They suggested that the attempt to destroy Europe's Jews could not be understood without noting the long history of anti-Semitism among Europeans. Anti-Semitic outlooks and religious discrimination were common practice in Europe since the Middle Ages, but became extreme once ethnicity and race were emphasized in the 1880s. Then racial anti-Semitism, and social resentment fuelled by Jewish professional successes in the post-emancipation era, added a new illiberal tone with petitions for quotas and citizenship restrictions. However, before World War I, the German situation seemed less tense than the French, with its Dreyfus case, in which an army officer's dismissal and banishment was based mainly on his Jewish background. Similarly, Russia had numerous pogroms, and Austria witnessed many violent attacks on individual Jews and savage interference with their ritual practices.

World War I changed the situation within Germany. Especially after Germany's defeat, the *völkisch* movements advocated a sorting of peoples by race. By then, conspiracy theories circulated that blamed a supposed international Jewish plot for Germany's loss of the war. Finally, in the 1920s, tracts such as the *Protocols of the Elders of Zion* – which alleged that an organized Jewish league sought to dominate the world – received a wide and sympathetic hearing.

The increased virulence of conspiratorial beliefs and anti-Semitic practice in Germany after World War I, including the racist elements of the Nazi Party program of 1920 and the fanatic beliefs of Adolf Hitler, were significant elements in the background to the Holocaust. Yet Nazi anti-Semitic convictions were deliberately restrained for electoral purposes prior to the party's gaining power in 1933. Some research has shown that support for the Nazis was not primarily for racial reasons, even if the idea of cleansing the body politic had wide support among health and medical professionals, as emphasized by Paul Weindling.[14] Yet handing the reins of power to Hitler and his followers was the necessary condition to setting Nazi Germany "on the twisted road to Auschwitz."[15]

Once Adolf Hitler had attained power, measures were taken against Jews and others identified as alleged threats to the national community (*Volksgemeinschaft*). Exclusionary measures were instituted against German Jews after 1933: economic boycotts, removal from state employment, limits to citizenship rights via the Nuremberg Laws of 1935, and the destruction of Jewish institutions. This all led to limiting of employment, undercutting of civic rights and even loss of life, especially during the *Kristallnacht* on November 9, 1938, when Jewish synagogues were burned in an officially organized and sanctioned pogrom. Due to the pressures placed on individuals and the Jewish community, more than half of Germany's Jews emigrated by 1939.[16]

---

14  See Paul Weindling, *Health, Race and German Politics between National Unification and Nazism, 1870–1945* (Cambridge: Cambridge University Press, 1989).

15  The thesis is in the title: Karl Schleunes, *The Twisted Road to Auschwitz: Nazi Policy toward German Jews, 1933–1939* (Urbana, IL: University of Illinois Press, 1970).

16  However, the practice of excluding Jews from German society operated with exceptions and contradictions. Some of the complexities, but especially the daily difficulties for Jews, appear in the recently published diaries of Victor Klemperer, an academic, who was not deported because his wife was not Jewish. Victor Klemperer, *I Will Bear Witness: A Diary of the Nazi Years, 1933–1941* (New York: Random House, 1998).

The Holocaust might be considered in stages. The Second World War brought a new, second stage, as Germany came into control of more than half of Poland, including nearly two million Polish Jews. In this stage, the circumstances for Jews in the newly occupied territories immediately became deplorable as life itself became dispensable. This new situation existed by late 1939 for two reasons: the concentration of Jews in ghettos and the beginnings of indiscriminate killing, which survivors' accounts have underscored. This stage was both arbitrary and planned in that the policies seemed to follow from earlier proclamations, but the practice was quite varied.

Another stage was reached after June 1941 with the introduction of three new types of killing that would be practised once the war against Russia began: (1) by *Einsatzgruppen*, the four main killing units that followed on the heels of German troops, their mission to destroy Jews and Soviet commissars; (2) by the six main killing centres, their purpose death on a mass scale, that became operational during 1942, and (3) by the so-called order police "actions." In the latter case, German police, made up mostly of reservists, sought out and systematically killed most of the remaining Jews in the villages and towns of Poland and the occupied eastern territories during 1942–44. The first two steps have been effectively explored by Raul Hilberg in his seminal study, *The Destruction of the European Jews*, in which he delineated in excruciating detail the process of concentrating and killing.[17] The latter stage has been illustrated graphically and in a nuanced fashion by Christopher Browning in his study, *Ordinary Men*.[18]

What makes the attempt to understand all the murdering more difficult is that during 1938–39 "actions" and a euthanasia program were undertaken against the *German* mentally and physically handicapped. And toward the end of the war there would follow senseless death marches of concentration camp inmates.

Incomprehension and puzzlement remains when discussing the Holocaust, its origins, and development. Since many of the great minds of the twentieth century have had difficulty arriving at firm conclusions about the sources and meaning of this dark historical chapter, it is not

17 Raul Hilberg, *The Destruction of the European Jews* (Chicago: Quadrangle Books, 1961; revised and expanded, 1985).

18 Christopher Browning, *Ordinary Men: Reserve Police Battalion 101 and the Final Solution in Poland* (New York: Aaron Asher Books, 1982).

surprising that no one has decisive or easy answers. The historians who have tried to come to terms with the crucial period 1941–45 have tried to make sense – just like the students – by examining antecedents, by combing through ideological beliefs, and by defining the institutional functioning of a system. The search for explanations for the origins of the Holocaust has divided historians into many camps, among which the functionalists emphasized the haphazard, unplanned aspects of bureaucratic endeavours while the intentionalists noted the plans and ideological purpose behind the military war. Similarly immense differences remain among scholars regarding intent and meaning, uniqueness and similarities with other genocides. The experts have provided many insights into who helped, who resisted, who planned, who perpetrated, and who stood by.[19] But their more objective voices cannot provide the human intensity of the victims' accounts.

## Memoirs

Many European Jews who survived the Holocaust have published memoirs of their experiences. Some wrote immediately after the events to bear witness, but they received little hearing from the public. By the mid-1990s, survivors' accounts numbered in the hundreds.

The memoir that follows is a gripping account of one person's experiences. Such accounts and accounting are crucial to seeing how the destructive process functioned and how some survived it. Perhaps the fullest answer to the question of how individuals could survive comes solely through memoirs, for instance those of Primo Levi, who does not make himself into a hero, but merely relates what occurred and draws some conclusions.[20]

Like other memoirs, those of Holocaust survivors raise questions of credibility and reliability of memory. At a methodological level, a critical analysis is required, because sources must be treated the same by historians

---

19 See Michael Marrus, *The Holocaust in History* (Toronto: Key Porter Books, 1987), and Donald L. Niewyk, ed., *The Holocaust: Problems and Perspectives of Interpretation* (Boston: Houghton Mifflin, 1997).

20 See Primo Levi, *Survival in Auschwitz: The Nazi Assault on Humanity* (New York: Collier Books, 1958), and, for example, Donald L. Niewyk, ed. *Fresh Wounds: Early Narratives of Holocaust Survival* (Chapel Hill: University of North Carolina Press, 1998), also some examples in Rita S. Botwinick, ed., *A Holocaust Reader* (Upper Saddle River, NJ: Prentice Hall, 1997).

regardless of the period and the event. For instance, most memoirs by politicians and military leaders – no matter in what time and what place – tend to offer only an apologia, but often they also offer a guide on where to look for more information. Others, such as some by German men and women who wrote soon after World War II, presented the end of the war and the ensuing occupation of Germany as a victimization of Germans. They presented themselves as refugees or as part of a world in which German "honour" seemed to be besmirched only with the arrival of Soviet troops. Such accounts need to be read for what they omit as well as what they present. Mostly, they offered only silence about the start of the war, the German rule over other peoples, the disappearance of their fellow citizens into concentration camps, or their turning away from what was happening all about them.

Holocaust survivors' memoirs also need to be examined for what individuals include or exclude, particularly whether pre-ghetto life is marked by class and gender differences. Most important, however, is to see the pattern of individual as well as representative experiences from 1939 to 1945. Not insignificant is the question of credibility and veracity: a few testimonials of Holocaust victims, individuals writing biographical histories for themselves, which cannot be verified or were found to be inaccurate, have underscored the importance of these attributes.

However, the great majority of memoirs, like the following, reinforce each other's claims of what happened and how. They provide insight into the pre-ghetto Polish world and how the war destroyed normal existence. An interesting comparison is with another survivor born in the same year, 1928, as Anna Heilman, namely Arthur Schaller.[21] Heilman's memoirs provide information on how women witnessed a different world than males in the ghetto, and especially in Auschwitz. And the following account provides – as does nearly every individual case – some novel elements. For instance, Heilman details the effect of decrees demanding the registration of pianos and what happened when the family tried to sell theirs. Novel, too, are her reflections recreated from memory based on diaries that were written in Auschwitz. This account reinforces the gender differentiation with which the Nazi overseers operated. Perhaps such memoirs, with their focus upon inhumane working conditions, allow comparisons with the conditions of early industrialization in Britain or with slavery, especially since the will to survive inhuman circumstances

---

21  See Arthur Schaller, *100 Cigarettes and a Bottle of Vodka: A Memoir* (Toronto: O. Lester Books, 1980).

here, too, led to resistance. Especially valuable is the new information on how the resisters obtained gunpowder at Auschwitz in 1944. Further, these memoirs should be considered in relation to other documents, such as *The Warsaw Diary of Adam Czerniakow* (who headed the Warsaw ghetto *Judenrat* until his suicide in July 1942)[22] or memoirs of other survivors, but they can stand on their own.

## Anna Heilman's Biography
## before and after Auschwitz

Anna Heilman was born on December 31, 1928, into a middle-class assimilated Jewish family in Warsaw, Poland. Her parents, Jacob and Rebecca, were both deaf (although all three of their children had normal hearing). Jacob was born in Warsaw in 1887. He owned a factory (Snycerpol) in Warsaw that employed deaf workers to make wooden handicrafts. He went to the Paris World Exposition to exhibit the factory's products in 1936. His products were also shown at the New York World's Fair in 1939. Rebecca was born in 1898 in Pruzany, Poland. She was from a wealthy family. Anna had two older sisters. Sabina, the eldest, escaped the Holocaust with her former tutor and future husband, Mietek. They survived by fleeing to the Soviet Union, and subsequently settled in Sweden.

Anna, her other sister Esther, and her parents lived in an apartment building at 38 Mila Street, in an area that became part of the Warsaw ghetto. Their building was down the street from 18 Mila Street, headquarters of the ZOB (*Zydowska Organizacja Bjojowa* – Jewish Fighting Organization), led by Mordecai Anielewicz. They were among the last to be deported from the Warsaw ghetto when they were taken to Majdanek in May 1943. Her parents were murdered upon arrival at Majdanek. Esther and Anna were sent to Auschwitz in September 1943.

Beginning in September 1943, Anna and Esther were "employed" as slave labourers in the Weichsel Union munitions factory at Auschwitz. Rather than submit willingly to the Nazis, knowing all the time that they were engaged in a virtually hopeless cause that could only end in their

---

22  Adam Czerniakow, *The Warsaw Diary of Adam Czerniakow: Prelude to Doom*, ed. Raul Hilberg, Stanislaw Staron, and Josef Kermisz; trans. Staron and the staff of Yad Vashem (New York: Stein & Day, 1979). On memoirs, see James Young, *Writing and Rewriting the Holocaust: Narrative and the Consequences of Interpretation* (Bloomington: Indiana University Press, 1988), and, on women, Carol Rittner and John Roth, *Different Voices: Women and the Holocaust* (New York: Paragon, 1993).

deaths, they and a small number of other women were involved in smuggling gunpowder from the factory to the men of the *Sonderkommando*. The conspirators figured that they would die anyway, but to participate in the uprising would give their deaths some meaning. The gunpowder was used to make explosives for use in the October 1944 uprising at Auschwitz.

After the uprising, Esther and three other young women were betrayed. After being horribly tortured, they were publicly executed before the whole camp on January 5, 1945. The execution occurred just before Auschwitz was brutally evacuated on January 18, 1945, as a result of the Soviet army's advance toward Germany. The four young women were murdered, as were millions of others, but their acts of defiance and courage forced the Nazis to recognize them as individuals. They were executed as resistance fighters under direct orders from Berlin.

Anna was sent on a forced march to Ravensbrück, where she stayed until February 1945, and then was at Neustadt-Glewe until being liberated by the Russians on May 2, 1945. After a brief stay in Belgium in May 1946, she emigrated to what was then Palestine.

Anna married Joshua Heilman on March 7, 1947. Joshua had left Poland to pursue his university studies one week before the outbreak of World War II. His younger sister Rose was also interned at Auschwitz, and survived the war. The rest of his family was murdered.

Anna obtained a degree in social work in Israel. Anna and Joshua had two daughters: Ariela, born in 1951, and Noa, born in 1953. Joshua went to the United States as a Hebrew teacher and brought the rest of the family to Boston in March 1958. In August 1960, the family emigrated to Ottawa, Canada, where Joshua found work as a Hebrew school principal. Anna worked with The Children's Aid Society in Ottawa as a bilingual (French/English) social worker until she retired as supervisor of the English/French unit in 1990. Anna and her husband live in Ottawa. Joshua continues to work as a translator for the Canadian government. Ariela lives in New York City with her husband and two children; Noa lives in Regina, Saskatchewan, with her husband and two children.

# Warsaw before World War II[1]

I loved our apartment. It was situated on the third floor of a three-storey building. The exterior was gray stone with elaborate cornices carved into half naked male statues, the locks of their hair crowned with laurel leaf wreaths. Urban Atlases, it looked like their broad shoulders supported the whole building.

You entered the complex through a massive iron gate consisting of two panels that could be opened inward to let a horse and buggy or a van through. Ordinarily, though, the gate was closed, and people entered through a door in the right-hand panel of the gate. Past the gate on the right was a door, which led to the apartments at the front of the building. This door also opened on a passage running the width of the building. The passage led to a rectangular courtyard. The larger apartments were at the front of the building, the smaller ones faced the courtyard. Our apartment was at the front of the building and had windows affording a view both of the street and of the courtyard.

To reach our apartment one had to climb wide, white marble stairs. A large window on each landing looked into the courtyard. The door to our apartment was of a heavy, red mahogany adorned with a gleaming brass plaque. Carved on the plaque in elaborate script was "J. Wajcblum" – my father, Jacob.

To the right of the door, also set in gleaming brass, was an electric doorbell. It was a magic bell. Every time one pushed the button, electric bulbs would light up in every room in the house to alert my parents, who were both deaf, that somebody was at the door.

It was totally dark as you entered the apartment. The front door opened into a long, narrow, and very dark corridor. A red oriental runner covered the herringbone-patterned wooden floor. On the right was my parents'

---

1  This chapter is a memoir. It was written between 1991 and 1994 in Ottawa, Canada.

bedroom, the double doors leading to it permanently closed. On the left was the door to our room, which we three girls grudgingly had to share. Farther down on the left were hangers upon hangers of outerwear: coats, hats, umbrellas, canes, and mittens. Trays on the floor held boots, street shoes; you name it, it was there.

This corridor was my private "hell-passage." The small lights set in fixtures way up in the ceiling did nothing to lighten the gloom of the long and dark corridor. Instead, the lights cast grotesque shadows. I used to run straight down the middle of the corridor, the coats and hats looming out at me, making me think that a mob of people was reaching out to grab me until I reached the last door on the left, which led to the kitchen.

The kitchen was large and bright, always filled with the wonderful smell of baking, cooking, or simmering food. In the kitchen was a large white table, a huge credenza that held pots and dishes and a bed in which our maid Warka slept, and a large coal "working stove" with white tiles over it. On the upper ledge of the tiles was a row of Droste cocoa boxes, which were used to hold all kinds of spices once the cocoa was finished.

I used to spend hours gazing at those boxes, examining them microscopically, particularly at the nurse painted on them, who held a tray with a box of Droste's cocoa. The pattern was infinitely repeated: the box on the tray in turn revealed a nurse holding a tray with a box of cocoa, and so on. I could never figure out how many nurses and boxes were painted on one box.

The bathroom lay at the very end of the corridor. Toward the end of the corridor on the right, just across from the kitchen was the combination living/dining room.

There were two walnut buffets in the dining room, decorated with carved leaves and flowers. One of the buffets had a beveled glass top over three lower doors. The top shelf held rainbow-coloured crystal bowls, goblets, and wine glasses from Belgium. Behind the bottom doors were the good china, silver, and all of my mother Rebecca's preserves. All the doors were locked, and my mother kept all the keys on a big ring attached to her belt.[2]

The dining room walls were decorated in a gold floral-patterned wallpaper, the flowers on delicate curved stems against a cobalt blue background. A narrow gold moulding framed the wallpaper, running all the way around the walls. Between the moulding and the ceiling was an eighteen-inch strip of plain cobalt blue wallpaper.

---

2  It seemed to be a custom that the woman of the house walked around locking everything. I think, in our case, it was to keep us out of the preserves.

On both walls adjoining the two buffets were oil paintings, two on each wall, that depicted the four seasons. My mother used to change them around, bringing the summer and spring paintings toward the middle of the room in wintertime, the winter and fall pictures in spring.

Between the window and the French door leading to the balcony stood a grandfather clock. Winding it was my father's responsibility. This wall and window were covered in plants.

There were eight chairs around the dining room table, heavy chairs with leather seats, beautifully carved to match the buffets. In addition to our family of six (including Isabella, our nanny), there was always company, so that all the chairs were always occupied. On Friday nights, my parents played cards, and the remaining four chairs, usually shoved against the walls beneath the pictures, would be pulled over to the table.

My parents and their friends loved to play cards. I always found it amazing how much noise the deaf can make when they are enjoying themselves.

To the left of the dining room was another set of French doors leading to my parents' bedroom. While my two older sisters Saba[3] and Estusia[4] did their homework in our room, I used to go in my parents' bedroom, stretch out on the ottoman, and watch the players through the open door.

My parents' bedroom was a sheer delight. The wallpaper was golden yellow inset with tiny blue rosebuds. Over my parents' two beds was a huge oil painting depicting a scene of victorious soldiers enjoying their "spoils of war" – women. The main figure was on horseback, holding in his arms a half-naked woman. I always feared that if the rearing horse's front hooves dropped, they would trample a group of women huddled together beside a little pond.

Behind the main figure were more soldiers, obviously having a lot of "fun." All the women were blond, blue-eyed and beautiful, dressed in gauzy dresses. The picture was so splendid in its execution that its sheer beauty overshadowed its somewhat scary subject matter.

The bedroom furniture was veneered in a blond wood. The vanity was curved, with two doors. The top of the vanity and its little companion bench were upholstered in pink and gold damask. The vanity upholstery was protected by a glass top. In the middle of the vanity was a long glassed drawer where my mother kept her toiletries in exquisite Limoges containers. The containers depicted eighteenth-century pastoral scenes,

---

3 A familiar form of her name, Sabina.

4 A familiar form of her name, Esther.

Anna's parents, Jacob and Rebecca Wajcblum

with romantic ladies and gentlemen clad in period clothing. Above the drawer was a triptych mirror. The mirrors on either side could be moved to afford a better side view.

There was a huge armoire, a mirror covering the middle door. In front of the armoire was a small round table, covered with the same pink and gold brocade under glass, and two tiny chairs with legs so spidery and frail-looking as if they would break if you sat on them. But they never did. The two chairs were upholstered in the same brocade.

Then there was the huge ottoman covered in hand-made oriental Gobelin silk. Gold arabesques and strange creatures were embroidered on its wine-coloured background. The ottoman was covered in cushions, all the fruit of my mother and Isabella's handiwork.

Anna's sister Saba, 1925/26

Behind the ottoman stood a four-paneled screen covering the permanently closed double doors leading into the corridor. The four panels were of hand-painted gold silk, featuring bright flowers, birds, and butterflies, all the work of my mother when she was younger.

On top of the armoire stood several demijohns, which contained my father's home-made *wisniak*.[5]

I loved being sick at home. The only time we could taste my father's delicious *wisniak* or my mother's preserves was when we were sick, or on special occasions when there was company for tea.

---

5 Cherry brandy.

The whole family gathered together at suppertime. My mother, the unquestioned empress of the house, presided over the meal, as she did over our entire house and our lives.

Tall, corpulent, blue-eyed, gray-haired, meticulously groomed, her ramrod posture made her appear even more formidable.

I knew that her posture was "helped" by a tightly laced corset, which I helped her put on in the morning and which she wouldn't take off until bedtime.

My mother would put on her corset and call me to tighten it for her. She would stand in front of the mirror at her vanity, holding onto it while directing me to tighten the laces.

*Tighter! Tighter!*

I had to pull the pink laces, put my knee to her back, and pull hard with both of my hands. She would then tie the ends in front of her waist, now no bigger than mine, her breasts way up, her back straight as a rod. I never knew how she could breathe and move in this armour.

We all had assigned places at the dining room table. My father sat at the head of the table, on my mother's right. Tall, slim, and very strong, he used to pick us up high in the air effortlessly. He had delicate features, and wore glasses over his deep-set brown eyes. He sported a small, military mustache. He always wore three-piece suits with high-collared shirts.

The shirts had no collars, really. The collars were separate, starched so heavily that they stood on their own and felt like cardboard. My father kept them in his night table, in cylindrical, highly lacquered sandalwood boxes. The boxes smelled wonderful. My father kept a watch with a gold chain in his vest's watch pocket.

My father owned a factory called Snycerpol. They made hand-carved wooden objects, for instance wooden plates with inscriptions on the rims such as "Give us our daily bread," wooden inkwells shaped like chestnuts resting on chestnut leaves, wooden pens with delicately carved animals on top, scores and scores of beautiful objects. My father employed only deaf-mute artisans, whom he picked up at their graduation from the Deaf-Mute Institute on 3 Crosses Square in Warsaw, his alma mater, and where he first met my mother.

To my mother's horror, my father was totally at ease with his deafness. He either couldn't or didn't try to lip-read; rather, his hands were in constant motion as he used them to talk.[6] He had beautiful hands with long fingers.

---

6 Both my parents were deaf from the ages of five years old. My mother had lost her hearing as a result of complications related to scarlet fever. My father lost his hearing as a result of an accident. In our home, we used sign language with both my parents. Outside

The tip of his left index finger was missing. He apparently lost it on an electric saw in the factory.

An artist in his own right, in addition to owning the factory, my father was also a representative of *Sztuka Ludowa Polska,*[7] and, as such, travelled a lot. Our house was a veritable museum of *objets d'art* that he collected abroad and brought home. In spite of being deaf, my father, self-taught, spoke fluent Polish, Russian, German, and Yiddish.

My father had a great sense of humour. He would amuse us with stories of his voyages to Belgium, to Russia, and once to Paris for the World's Fair.

He used to make us laugh so hard that Estusia, laughing with her mouth full, would always spill something on the tablecloth. My mother would become furious and tell my father to stop talking, but it never helped – Estusia sat across and down the table from my mother, at a safe distance. On the other hand, when I laughed, my mother would poke me in the ribs. I used to sit on her left at the dining table, so that she could keep an eye on me. I think that I had a permanent ache on my right from her poking.

I loved the story my father used to tell about his travels deep into Asian Russia: One day, he went into a teahouse. Inside were long wooden tables with benches on each side. Strangers sat next to one another on these benches. It was very cold outside that day, and the place was full of customers who had come in to warm up. To order tea, one gave a coin to the man watching the smoking samovar at the head of the table. He would fill a cup with boiling tea, and the other customers would pass the cup to the one who had paid. To sweeten their tea, the customers licked sugar from heavy cones weighing about two kilograms each, that hung from the ceilings.

My older sister Saba sat to my father's right. She had hazel eyes and straight brown hair, a source of much misery, as her hair would not respond to Isabella's daily ministrations of the curling iron. Saba always seemed to be in a bad mood and had little patience for her younger sisters.

As the oldest, Saba was my parents' right arm, their spokesman to the outside world. They both depended heavily on her speaking ability. As such, she held a privileged position within the family constellation, and reserved for herself a special status. In my parents' eyes, she was always right.

---

the house, I used sign language with my father and lip reading with my mother. My mother was very vain and self-conscious about her handicap. As she spoke only Russian, I had to interpret Polish to her whenever we were together in shops, etc. While my father could speak, his speech was not very distinct and had the monotonic guttural quality of the deaf. In contrast, my mother's speech was clearer.

7 Polish Folk Art Organization.

The three sisters (left to right):
Anna, Sabina, and Estusia, 1933.

All three of us girls shared the same bedroom, which contained only one desk. As with all desks, the only good place was in the middle, where there was space to put your knees under the desktop. On the right side were three open shelves. This side was second best, because you could put your feet on the bottom shelf and your knees would fit into the space between the bottom shelf and the next shelf up. The left side was the worst.

Sometimes we would make deals among ourselves. The first one at the desk after supper could have the middle seat.

It never failed: should Estusia or I get there first, Saba would run to complain to my mother. My mother would unceremoniously order us to the sides. The desk was big enough for the three of us, but the humiliation and injustice of the situation rankled deeply. Needless to say, Saba's attitude did not endear her to us. This pushed Estusia and me into a conspiratorial alliance against her.

We used to fight and scream obscenities at each other – with impunity, because our parents couldn't hear. Warka, our maid, who *could* hear, chose instead to play deaf rather than interfere. When we heard our mother's approach by the clinking of her keys (the carpets muffled her footsteps), we would jump to our seats, three angels hard at work.

On the right of Saba at the dining room table sat Estusia. Her face was all huge green eyes. She had a mass of wavy chestnut hair that was braided into either one or two thick braids hanging down her back. She ate like a horse, but she was skinny, all dangling arms and long legs.

We used to make fun of her and call her "Sucha Regina," which is translated as "dried-out prune." Estusia and I were pals. We kept each other's secrets, or more accurately, Estusia could depend on me to keep her secrets.

We did a lot of things together.

The parquet floor in our dining room was made of three shades of wood, laid in a repeating pattern of four small squares framed by wooden strips to make a large square, kind of like a four-paned window. If you squinted a little bit, you couldn't tell which small squares combined to create which big squares.

Anyway, it was perfect for hopscotch. We used to hop and skip on it for hours. There was plenty of room between the dining room table and the grand piano that took up almost the entire living room. (Saba used to play this piano.) Then to cover the scuff marks we would polish the waxed floor with a special polishing broom. It had hard, short bristles and ran on ball bearings.

We used to take turns riding on the broom, holding the handle, while the other would pull and push back and forth to polish the floor. One day, Estusia was giving me a ride. She didn't notice the chair behind her. Banging into it, her arm carried on by the momentum, she punched herself in the mouth, knocking out one of her front teeth.

When my mother came home, she was beside herself with grief and rage. Nothing more dreadful could happen to a girl than to have her front tooth knocked out! We were so afraid of my mother that, despite Estusia's actual pain and my sympathy for it, we forgot to cry.

The next day, the three of us went to the dentist. We sat on hard wooden chairs in the waiting room. The walls were decorated with pictures of sad-looking animals, tears dropping from their eyes, their jaws bandaged by kerchiefs knotted on top of their heads. From inside the doctor's office we heard the screaming of a patient under treatment.

Estusia and I wanted to run away. My mother, of course, could hear none of it. She didn't do a thing. She didn't even move. She just glared at us from behind her magazine. That was enough.

Finally, Estusia was fitted out with a new tooth that was attached to her gum on a shaft. If you didn't know, you couldn't tell the difference.

On Estusia's right at the dining room table sat Isabella, our nanny. She was always there for us. Isabella had brown eyes and plucked eyebrows that always gave her a surprised expression. She carefully waved her brown hair with a curling iron. (This curling iron was a permanent fixture on our kitchen stove. Somebody was always using it, mostly to curl their hair, except for me, for whom it was used to straighten my hair).

Isabella was slim, graceful, and sinuous. I think that it was Isabella who inspired Estusia to dance and both of us to excel in gymnastics. She could twist her body into the most impossible contortions. She could even fit her foot into our small shoes.

Like my mother, she always wore high heels; even her slippers at home had high heels. Isabella knew how to do everything. She could sew, she could knit, she could crochet. She taught me how to make exquisite paper doilies with scissors. She would cuddle us, spoil us, and I know that, although she loved us all, I was her favourite.

Our morning started with breakfast, Warka, our maid, busy in the kitchen. My mother never got up until everybody was already out, but Isabella was under strict orders not to let anybody get up from the table until the food on their plate was finished. My father left for work at his factory, Saba and Estusia left for school. I was always left the last and only one at the table.

I hated porridge. No matter how much butter and sugar was added, I couldn't stand the look of the gluey mess. Finally, taking pity on me, or maybe impatient to catch up with her schedule, Isabella used to finish it for me and I was allowed to leave the table.

My mother liked fresh air so much that she kept all the windows in our apartment open winter, spring, and fall. They were only closed during the summer, when we were not there. Because my mother liked fresh air, Isabella had to take me out every winter morning for a sled ride. Isabella would bundle me up in my white rabbit-fur coat with a matching hat, tied with a ribbon under my chin, white rubber overshoes, white woolen mitts that Isabella knitted, so that finally I resembled a snowball. She would put on her black cloth coat with a brown fox collar and her inevitable cloche hat. She wore high-heeled boots that reached to mid-calf.

We would go all the way down to the basement storage area where my sled was kept. It took some years before I could run down the white marble stairs without needing to hold onto the banister. As it was, Isabella had to wait for me while I stepped down with both feet on each step, holding onto her hand while she held the banister. There was no elevator in our building, and as we had to go all the way from the third floor, our descent took a long time.

Finally downstairs, she would take out my sled. It looked like a curved-back rocking chair. It was cozy and comfortable with a pillow behind my head and back. A soft, heavy blanket was wrapped all around me up to my chin. I kept my hands underneath it. But I was still freezing. I cried all the way there and back on my sled ride.

I think that Isabella must have hated these daily outings as much as I did. No amount of distraction would stop my crying. She would point out the gay horse-driven sleighs, the horses decorated with red, blue, green, yellow, and white plumes, the bells hanging around their necks tinkling merrily. In spring and summer, the coachmen would take off the metal runners that glided so smoothly on the hard beaten snow and replace them with wheels, thus transforming the sleighs into calèches.

Isabella would stop in front of the shop windows to look at the displays. The windows were covered with frost except at the very bottoms, where there were long gas pipes with tiny holes. The flickering blue gas flames melted the frost and enabled pedestrians to view the wares displayed at the bottom of the windows. Usually I would be fascinated with the variety of treasures displayed there. But not in winter.

Finally, we would return home, where Isabella would dry my tears with kisses, warm my numb hands in her armpits, and rub my feet with her hands. Isabella was my constant companion. She, like my parents, was deaf. She had been my mother's schoolmate from their days at the Warsaw Institute for the Deaf. Isabella was Catholic; we were Jewish.

Although she was in our home constantly, Isabella did not live with us. She had her own apartment, which I don't remember ever visiting. It was Isabella who introduced me to church. I loved the lofty space of the church, dark, illuminated only by the brightly coloured stained glass windows. The sunlight brought the colours and designs to life, but did not penetrate the gloom inside. The only other lighting came from dim electric lamps high up in the ceilings. Set in wrought-iron baskets, their only contribution was to light the ceiling. One had to wait for a few minutes to get adjusted to the dark interior.

Another source of light was the rows and rows of candles lit under the statues of the Virgin Mary holding baby Jesus in her arms. The church smelled sweetly of burning incense. Sometimes an organ would be playing, but most often it was very still. I loved the serene atmosphere of the church.

It imposed a hush and reverence upon you. Nobody had to explain it to me. Isabella would kneel and pray, and I would just sit quietly beside her looking at the beautiful statues and pictures all around.

It was Isabella again who introduced me to the cinema. I remember going with her to see the Little Rascals. She bought tickets at the booth outside the cinema.

Sparkling, cascading chandeliers illuminated the ceilings and the two storeys of carved gingerbread balconies and loges. I was enchanted. I thought it was beautiful. There were rows and rows of red plush chairs that sprung up as soon as you left your seat. You had to pull them down with your hands and sit quickly or they would spring up again.

Then the lights would go out, and a newsreel came on before the movie. Then came the main feature. On screen, people were pushing, pulling, and running, to the accompaniment of organ music played to match the mood of the action. It didn't surprise me that there was no sound coming from the screen. After all, in our house people communicated more through sign language and facial expressions than through spoken language.

Isabella, deaf, laughed so hard that tears flowed down her cheeks. I jumped up and down in my seat, responding not only to the action on the screen but to the enthusiastic shrieks of the audience, who screamed with delight as they encouraged the boys' antics or booed the villains. And every time I jumped up I was squeezed by the spring-loaded seat and had to push it all the way back to get it to lie flat again. It was wonderful.

One day, a new movie theatre called the Palladium opened in Warsaw. Isabella talked my mother into coming with us to see a Shirley Temple movie. I was disappointed with the theatre itself. It did not have plush seats, or gingerbread balconies, or crystal chandeliers. It had hidden soft lighting that would appear and disappear gradually as if by magic. There was not a bulb in sight. By comparison, the Palladium was austere, but its screen was much bigger and the movie had sound. Mother and Isabella were very impressed. I cried and laughed in sympathy with Shirley Temple's changing fortunes.

When we got back home, Isabella and mother decided that I should wear clothes just like Shirley Temple. Isabella was a seamstress *par excellence*, my mother the designer. Off came the gorgeous tablecloth from our dining room table, revealing the pad that protected the tabletop. Isabella and mother got busy with scissors and newspapers and started making paper patterns. They cut, they measured, they fit the paper on me, and finally they started to cut the material. They stood me on a little stool and had me stand for hours, looking critically, ordering me to turn around.

Slowly, too much! Too little! More to the left! More to the right!

The final result was a navy blue coat with a Peter Pan collar and one row of buttons from top to bottom, just covering my behind, and a matching round hat with a small rim and navy blue silk ribbon band ending in two strands on the back, about three inches long. Mother and Isabella were very proud of their handiwork, and so was I. But secretly I found two major flaws with it: it had no pockets and no belt.

Before I started school, I used to go shopping with my mother, trips that were both an agony and an ecstasy.

My mother did not walk across the street, she sailed, looking neither right nor left, oblivious to the traffic, deaf to the cursing of calèche drivers, the honking and sudden braking of the taxis, the clang of the streetcars' ringing bells.

She expected the traffic to stop; it did. In the meantime, as I died a thousand deaths, she impatiently shrugged off my tugs on her coat in an effort to get her to stop.

She was a very picky shopper; each item seemed to have to come from a different store. In one shop we bought her special brand of coffee beans to be ground and brewed at home; her special tea came from a different shop, herring from still another. Buying a few groceries literally involved criss-crossing the whole of Warsaw.

No shopping trip would be complete without a visit to the Hale (Hale Mirowskie). The Hale was a gigantic indoor market, a long building with a glass roof, where they sold meat, fish, fruit, and vegetables. Inside, the wide main passage branched into a maze of narrow side aisles off which were rows and rows of stalls. The largest, best-illuminated stalls were situated on the main passage.

All sorts of smells permeated the air, and the asphalt floor was always wet and slippery from the constant washing and spraying required to keep the produce fresh. As a result, walking was quite hazardous. Because of the abundance of pickpockets, the shoppers, mostly women, held tightly onto their bags and wallets.

The Hale sold produce from all over Poland and from most of Europe. The meat stores had hooks in the ceiling from which hung rabbits, chickens, ducks, and geese. The birds could be bought either dressed or with the plumage still on. Behind the birds hung suckling pigs. The back wall was "decorated" with hanging sides of beef.

The fish stores featured all kinds of freshwater fish and seafood from the Baltic Sea. The fish was sold fresh or smoked. The smoked varieties were displayed in flat wooden boxes or in small wooden barrels. You could buy them either by weight or by the box. They sold smoked and fresh eel, smoked salmon, flounder, carp, sprats, tiny smoked sardines, and a larger variety of smoked herring.

My mother used to buy all kinds of smoked fish and fresh flounder. She would also buy carp and pike to make gefilte fish[8] for the Friday Sabbath supper.

There were also cheese stalls where they sold huge, flat wheels of Swiss cheese, red balls of gouda from Holland, smelly, delicious Limburger cheese from Germany, blue cheeses, an endless variety. Soft Greek cheeses and goat cheese hung from the ceilings. They looked like fat wine bottles, suspended by eight strands of string joined together by a knot on top.

The most beautiful cheeses came from the Polish Tatry mountains in the Carpathians. These were made in the winter by shepherds tending their flocks in the mountains. They looked like two cones joined together at the base. They were black on the outside as a result of the shepherds' smoking them over open fires and were decorated with geometrically carved patterns. When sliced open, they were milky white, semi-soft, with a characteristic mild goat cheese flavour. Delicious!

After the Hale, we would buy dry goods. My favourite shop was a sewing supplies store where they sold notions, such as buttons, ribbons, and needles. They had many, many different varieties of buttons and my mother would spend hours choosing the ones that pleased her.

My sisters and I used to wear ribbons everywhere – on our heads, on our collars, sometimes as belts to match the ribbons in our hair. They were made of taffeta and came in all the colours of the rainbow – in both solid colours and plaid patterns – and all widths, some as narrow as a shoelace, some as wide as seven inches and everything in between. The shop also carried all kinds of lace, ivory fans, and collars. Many of the collars were lacy, or made of stringed beads in many different colours. Mother would mostly choose white pique collars for us, bordered in narrow lace. She would also buy us sailor collars, navy blue with three rows of white silk ribbon sewn on them.

I also liked to go to the shoe store. They had an X-ray machine that showed our toes inside the shoe, so that if we didn't like the look of the shoes, we couldn't "cheat" and claim that shoes we didn't like were too big or too tight. We were never consulted on choice and seldom listened to.

Weather permitting, we would then go and sit in an outdoor café. Novy Swiat was one of the main arteries of Warsaw, featuring cafés and mouth-watering patisseries. My mother loved to be looked at and to look at the passers-by.

---

8  Gefilte fish (literally "filled fish") is stewed or baked fish made from fish, bread crumbs, eggs and spices. Gefilte fish is formed into balls or ovals.

For a long time, I thought that everybody knew my mother, because the gentlemen passing by would tip their hats to her; it was only much later that I realized it was customary and polite for gentlemen to tip their hats to attractive ladies. My mother basked in this show of homage and returned it with brilliant smiles. As for the lady passers-by, my mother kept up a running commentary, mostly critical.

*Look at this one, she looks like a peacock! And this one! Can you imagine wearing green with her complexion? Look at those shoes, where did she get them, at the second-hand store? ...*

My mother considered herself the ultimate authority on matters of fashion, taste, and the latest styles. This was reinforced by the attitude of sales clerks, who would run towards her when she would grace their stores. The shopkeepers knew my mother and deferred to her.

They were eager to please my mother because they knew she had a wide circle of friends and relatives who would not buy a stitch of apparel without her advice. And if they did buy something without her advice, and my mother did not like it, she wouldn't hesitate to go back to the offending store and berate the salespeople for selling such an unsuitable thing to her friends.

So the shopkeepers would run to bring their best chairs for her to sit on, and she would hold court, choosing the latest styles and colours. She did not need me as a translator; the salespeople were her contemporaries[9] whom she could lip-read flawlessly.

We would return home by calèche because invariably the parcels were too numerous and too heavy for us to walk home with.

On Sundays, we used to go to gather chestnuts with Isabella at the Catholic cemetery on Powazki. It was beautiful: the graves were adorned with marble angels, the mausoleums with their miniature wrought-iron fences resembled little palaces. Everything was under a canopy of tall trees. It was very quiet there, and chestnuts lay all around. When fresh, the chestnuts glistened with a shiny reddish-brown colour, the same colour as the squirrels that fled from us.[10] Some chestnuts were still in their green spiky outer shells. These we crushed open carefully with the heel of our shoes, so as not to damage the chestnuts inside. These chestnuts looked like spotted brown and white ponies. With time, they would darken all brown and harden until they were like stones.

---

9   That is, they spoke Russian. At the time my parents were going to school, the Russians controlled eastern Poland and the language of instruction was Russian.

10   The squirrels in Poland were red. Hence the Polish expression "ruddy as a squirrel."

We would play with them for hours at home. We would string them into long necklaces, make reins out of them, and play horses. Or we would carve them and, with wooden matches, make doll furniture out of them. My father would make glue out of them. When they were old and dry, my mother would burn them with coal in the tall, white-tiled stoves that were used to heat our apartment. When they burned, they would explode with noises like pistol shots.

If we didn't go to Powazki, we would frequent one of the many parks in Warsaw. The one nearest us was Traugutt Park, which contained an old Russian citadel. We used to run and climb its tall ramparts.

In winter, we used to skate on the lake in Saski Park. We would watch the swans and ducks swimming in the lake before it froze. The palace wasn't open to the public, but the garden was. For a few cents, you could rent a chair to sit on if all the benches were occupied.

The park maintenance workers were municipal employees. They wore caps featuring a mermaid, Warsaw's official emblem. They walked around armed with sticks with a nail at the bottom. The sticks were used to pick up stray leaves and pieces of paper. They were a grumpy, ill-tempered lot, always chasing children off the grass and threatening them with their sticks if found littering.

But the most beautiful park was Lazienki. While we could walk to the other parks, we had to take a long tram ride to Lazienki. The tram would take us from the Royal Square of the Royal Palace (the residence of the Polish president Moscicki) through the Krakowskie Przedmiescie.[11] Palaces belonging to the nobles and Polish aristocracy lined either side of the boulevard.

Then the tram went through the university. It was housed in a complex of palaces, which through the centuries had belonged to a succession of Polish kings and which had been donated to the university.

From there, it was on to Nowy Swiat[12] Boulevard, lined on both sides by patisseries, shops, and outdoor cafés, then on to Aleje Ujazdowskie. This boulevard was divided in the middle by a median on which grew lush and leafy chestnuts. On the right were old mansions, smaller than the palaces but no less imposing, which housed some of the wealthy Polish aristocracy and foreign embassies. The left side was wholly occupied by a complex of many palaces in the great Ujazdowski Park.

---

11  Royal Way.

12  New World.

On the very north was situated the Belvedere, the residence of Marshal Joseph Pilsudski.[13] Inside the park was the Lazienki palace. The Lazienki dominated the smaller temples and monuments hidden all through the park among the trees. There was a rectangular reflecting pool in front of the palace. We used to bring crusts of bread to feed the swans in the pool.

For a small fee the palace was open to the public. Inside you could view art of the Middle Ages, Impressionist painters, and the massive epic canvas of Jan Matejko, one of the most famous Polish painters. Also on display were period furniture, tapestries, and precious vases and china from all over the world. Large and beautiful as the palace was, it was difficult to find, hidden behind the trees in the vast expanse of the park. We had to keep close to Isabella or my mother, whoever it was that accompanied us, because it was very easy to get lost in the maze of pathways. There were several gates to the park, and at the gates were kiosks selling souvenirs, postcards, and sweets.

An exception to my mother's rules against buying junk on the street, Isabella would buy us treats there. Our favourites were Pischinger rum balls from Germany. These were chocolate-covered waffle balls with a delicious soft chocolate filling. Inside each ball were hidden treasures: miniature glass animals made from coloured opaque glass, frogs, cats, dogs, turtles, wrapped tightly in cellophane. We each had a collection of these animals. Another favourite was chocolate-covered "bananas." These were banana-shaped chocolates with a soft yellow filling that tasted like bananas.

In November, we used to go to the Jewish cemetery on Okopowe.[14] It wasn't nearly as nice as the Catholic one. First of all, there were no trees there. And there were no angels. The graves were mostly modest stones, curved on top, featuring two palms with extended fingers touching each other, or a little pitcher dripping drops of stone-carved oil. There were some family mausoleums with elaborate lions and fishes carved on them, but they were few and far between.

My mother used to buy big bouquets of yellow and white chrysanthemums and lay them on the graves of both of my grandfathers.[15] My mother's father, Jankiel-Shyma Jaglom, died before I was born, so I never knew him. But his memory was kept alive by the large portrait of

---

13  This palace was destroyed during the war, but was subsequently rebuilt.

14  As I later found out, it was a Polish Catholic, not a Jewish, custom to visit the cemetery for All Soul's Day on November 2.

15  This is also a Polish, not a Jewish, custom.

him that hung in our living room, on the wall above the piano. My father's father died when I was about seven years old. I do remember him. His name was Shiye Wajcblum. My grandparents lived in Warsaw on Stawki Street, number 19, in an apartment over the street-level floor occupied by my father's factory.

When not shopping or going with Isabella to parks, I would spend my time kneeling on the sofa in our room, my elbows on the window sill and my nose and forehead pressed against the windowpane. The windows in our room faced the courtyard, which always teemed with a life of its own. It had a rhythm and timetable as predictable as the seasons of the year. Like waves on the sea, it was always the same yet forever changing.

The courtyard was enclosed on all four sides by the apartment complex. Summer or winter, all the windows were opened early in the morning and all the bedding hung out over the window sills to air.

Later in the morning it was time for people to beat their rugs. In each corner of the courtyard[16] were two poles, about seven or eight feet tall and about eleven or twelve feet apart. A wooden bar stretched between the poles. The rugs would be thrown across the bar and the maids would beat them vigorously and rhythmically.

Beating the rugs and the subsequent reaction constituted the two acts of a daily performance that never changed. Accompanied by much yelling and cursing, people would frantically remove all the bedding from the windows, to avoid their being covered by the clouds of dust that flew upward as a result of the rug beating.

I don't know what or who organized the rug-beating schedule for the complex. The four sets of poles had to serve the forty-eight families living in our apartment complex, and I don't remember any line-ups.

When our rugs needed beating, I remember Warka making several trips to the poles, the rugs thrown over her shoulders. She was "armed" with a rug beater made from dried willow branches. Somewhat rounder and with bigger holes than a tennis racket, the rug beater consisted of a long handle and a flat scrolled surface.

Warka was a sturdy, tall girl of peasant stock. She must have been nineteen or twenty when she first joined our family. She had red cheeks; brown, smiling eyes; and abundant brown hair, which she used to braid and wind around her head into a crown. Warka came to us from Pruzany in eastern Poland. My mother brought her back to Warsaw from one of

---

16 This naturally meant that lower apartments near the poles were much less desirable than higher or more distant apartments.

our summer trips to visit my maternal grandmother.[17] I remember that by the time Warka came to us the cobblestones in the courtyard had been covered with asphalt and were smoother to walk on.

Joining us in the metropolis of Warsaw was Warka's first venture out of her sleepy little town. It used to amuse us children to see her startle at the urban noises – the streetcars, the jostling humanity. We had to take turns escorting her around, to help her get accustomed to the sounds and familiarized with the geography so that she wouldn't get lost.

· One day, Warka was very unhappy. She was convinced that she had developed a terminal disease, and asked Saba's advice. Upon examination, Saba saw that Warka had dandruff.

Saba, with her peculiar sense of humour, told Warka with a straight face that indeed, it was a *very* serious case of dandruff. In fact, Saba "knew" of a woman who had died from having dandruff under her armpits. Warka burst into tears, inconsolable.

When my mother found out, she was furious with Saba for being so cruel, but, averting her face, she laughed too. The problem was solved very quickly by rinsing Warka's hair with camomile tea. The tea acted as a water softener to combat the effects of Warsaw's hard water.

Later in the morning after the rug beating, all kinds of peddlers would come by, each one having their own particular style and method of advertising their trade or wares.

There was the potato-peel buyer who advertised his trade in sing-song Yiddish. My mother told me that the peels were used to fatten pigs. The glazier came by, a wooden frame on his back holding his glass. The knife and scissors sharpener would arrive on a tricycle, ringing bells to announce his entrance.

Then there was the tin man. He was a very important fellow. Most kitchen utensils were made of tin. The dishes were washed in large tin bowls and then dried on a wicker basket perched on another tin bowl to catch the drips. Cooking pots were made of enameled tin. They used to spring leaks from constant use, so the tin man's services were always very much in demand.

Then there were the rag men. They intrigued and scared me the most. I wondered which one of them was the disguised wizard who bought Aladdin's magic lamp.

---

17  We spent our summers first at my maternal grandmother's home in Pruzany, my mother's birthplace. Later, we spent our summers in Druskieniki. Druskieniki was a resort town in northeast Poland, situated near the river Niemen, which constituted the border between Poland and Lithuania. It is now in Lithuania.

Afternoon was entertainment time. Groups of gypsies used to come with fiddles and cymbals to sing, dance, perform acrobatics, and to tell fortunes by reading cards. Warka would often sneak out to have the cards read to her. Invariably she would return with a dreamy and beatific expression on her face. She would firmly believe that a fortune was coming to her in the near future, along with a dark and handsome man to woo her for her hand in marriage.

Then the organ grinder would come to play his tinny music, a colourfully clad monkey perched on his shoulder. The monkey had a little tambourine with tiny cymbals on its edges, which it used to catch the coins thrown down by the people watching from their windows. The monkey would constantly turn its head from side to side, up and down, its eyes darting and scanning. At the first sign of any movement, the monkey would jump off the man's shoulder and deftly catch the coins in his tambourine.

I would run madly into the kitchen and pester Warka to give me a coin. I would then carefully wrap the coin in a piece of old newspaper, so it wouldn't get lost, and wave my arms wildly to catch the monkey's attention, to get it closer to my side of the building. If the monkey succeeded in catching the coin in its tambourine, which it most often did, I would clap my hands in excitement, and so would the other spectators.

Still later in the day, children would take over the courtyard as their playground. They would use the rug-beating poles as gym equipment, climbing up, swinging precariously from the bar, and jumping down. They ran after a tireless bicycle wheel, using a wire bent into a hook to balance the wheel, which created a raucous clatter. It was a poor man's version of the wooden wheel-and-stick toy which my father manufactured in his factory, and which I played with in the park. The children would also play tag, hide and seek, hopscotch, and ball. The girls concentrated on jumping rope and playing ball games.

There seemed to be an infinite variety of ball games. One of the most popular was a variant of wall ball with progressive levels of difficulty. First, the ball was thrown against the wall to be caught seven times without a bounce. Then you had to catch it six times with one bounce, then standing on one foot, then the other, then with one hand, then the other, then last, and most difficult, throw the ball, turn around and catch it before it hit the ground. These games were accompanied by the sounds of both delight and dispute.

The boys' favourite game was to use a stick to flick a little wooden peg up in the air, and before it could fall, bat it far away with the stick. The sticks were also often used to settle disputes.

I envied the children's fun and games, never being able to join them since my mother didn't believe in mixing with the "rough" crowd. Even though all the children came from the same apartment complex, she referred to them as "street kids."

So I remained a spectator. But the children were familiar with my face in the window. They knew my name and I knew some of theirs. We shouted each other's names. They would yell to me to come and join them. Sometimes, I used to sneak down when my mother was away. But I was uneasy in my play. I was afraid of being found out by my mother, and since I didn't play with them often, I wasn't fully accepted as one of them.

However, I soon found another way to be a participant rather than a passive observer. One day, my father gave me his coin collection to play with.

I caught the eye of a boy and motioned him to go to the front of the building, on the street side. While he ran there, I ran to the front balcony and threw him a coin. In a flash, a whole pack of children ran after him, and they began fighting for the coins.

It didn't take long for our concierge to find out what had made the children run wild. He complained to my father, who confiscated the coin collection. My parents, feeling that something had to be done about me, decided that I was old enough to start school. Still a five-year-old, I would normally have been considered too young to start school that year. I only turned six in December 1934, which was past the "cut-off date" for starting school.

At first, the school authorities refused to take me because I was too young, but since we were all going to a private, all-girls Catholic school, they accepted me conditionally. If I did not measure up, they would send me home. I was very excited at the prospect of starting school, and very much aware of the condition. I measured up.

Isabella sewed my school uniform – a black alpaca, long-sleeved frock, with a white Peter Pan collar. It buttoned down the front and was worn on top of our ordinary clothes. As always, my mother added the inevitable bow to the front of the collar. My father presented me with a beautiful brown leather schoolbag.

So one September morning, flanked by Saba on one side and by Estusia on the other, we all boarded the streetcar and my school career started.

I had a few obstacles to overcome. Some children are naturally neat, some manage to find dirt where there is none. I was in the last category. Invariably, by the time I got back from school, my black frock was covered with white chalk and my white collar was black with grime, the bow missing.

My teacher introduced me to the class as the new student and asked me to say my name; I proudly said, "Anusia." That is what I was called at home. My teacher said that "Anusia"[18] was a baby name. So from that day on I became Hanka.

My teacher sent a note to my mother suggesting that it was not customary to curl girls' hair. There was nothing my mother could do about it, so she sent a note back to my teacher telling her that my hair was naturally curly. Neither was pleased.

Surrounded in my class by blond, blue-eyed girls, I was conspicuous by my dark complexion and curly black hair. I remember that, even though most people said I had nice eyes, I used to wash my eyes with soap because somebody at school had said that I had "dirty eyes." I didn't look like anybody, not like anybody at school, not like anybody in my family.

My mother used to tease me, saying that she stole me from a gypsy camp. I believed her for many years. When I was mad at her I used to fantasize that I really was an adopted child and that one day I would find my real parents and run away from home.

My mother didn't believe in an allowance or pocket money. She felt that whatever we needed we had at home, and what we didn't have we shouldn't have. So to give ourselves allowances, Estusia and I would pocket the streetcar fare she gave us and instead run to school. We knew by heart the shortcuts through the courtyards and all the hidden passageways.[19]

Then we would cross the Krasinski Garden. It was named after the Polish Count Krasinski, whose imposing white palace stood on the grounds. Though the park was public, the palace was not. It was not a museum either, unlike Lazienki Palace. Krasinski Garden was large and beautiful. Like all the parks in Warsaw, it boasted massive and majestic chestnut, oak, and maple trees.

Sometimes there was a heavy fog on our morning hikes to school. It was like walking through a thick milky wall that magically disappeared when you approached it. You couldn't see more than a few feet ahead. Estusia used to frighten me by disappearing in the dense fog. I would call to her in a panic, and she would answer like a ship's foghorn, and I had to follow the sound.

From Krasinski Garden, it was a short hop to number 14 Miodowa Street where our school, *Wspolpraca*, was located.

---

18 Though "Anusia" was not acceptable, "Estusia" (Esther) never seemed to be in question. I don't know whether "Anusia" was out of bounds because of my teacher's particular distaste for the name or because "Estusia" seemed to be a relatively common name in its own right, while "Anusia" wasn't.

19 This knowledge was later to save our lives.

We always beat the streetcar and were at school on time. The way back home was an orgy of gorging ourselves with chocolate. On Senatorska Street, there was a fancy candy and chocolate store called Helvetia. They had all kinds of handmade chocolates shaped according to the season – Santas at Christmas and Easter eggs at Easter. They had mouth-watering truffles and marzipan fruits and vegetables that looked real. They had miniature pastel mints and glazed fruit half-covered in dark chocolate. Best of all, they had small cellophane bags with red ribbons that contained broken pieces of chocolate and other goodies, not fit to sell to regular customers, but what a treasure for us! The cost was the equivalent of a dime. We used to take our time walking back home, making the chocolate last as long as possible. It never spoiled our appetite for dinner.

Often my father would come home at night with bagels worn like bracelets on both his coat sleeves. The bagels were sold on street corners by vendors who shouted out their wares. They were kept in big wicker baskets covered in cloth to keep them warm and moist. They were hot and fragrant, baked just in time for supper. The tops were braided and covered with coarse salt crystals and poppy seeds. Purchasing bagels off the street scandalized my mother, and, though we just couldn't wait to bite into them, we had to wait until my mother "disinfected" them by burning off the germs on the hot iron top of the kitchen stove.

In September or October (the Gregorian date varied because the holidays are determined according to the lunar-based Hebrew calendar), we celebrated Rosh Hashanah.[20]

My parents put on their finest clothes to go to the synagogue, my mother in her Persian lamb fur coat and matching hat, my father wearing gloves and carrying a silver-handled cane to complement his bowler hat. He wore a black coat with a brown fur collar. The coat was lined in black and white fur. I could smell the wonderful scent of my mother's perfume as she bent to kiss us goodbye. For once, my father looked very solemn. Off they went.

Estusia told me that Rosh Hashanah was an important Jewish holiday. Seven days later was Yom Kippur.[21]

My father put a long wax candle in a flowerpot and lit it before leaving for the synagogue, admonishing us not to go near it. This candle was supposed to burn for twenty-four hours. Both my parents had tears in their eyes as they left for the synagogue.

---

20  The Jewish New Year.

21  The Jewish Day of Atonement.

Estusia said that you are supposed to cry and fast on Yom Kippur. I tried to cry but it didn't come, and as for fasting, I could smell the delicious dinner that Warka was cooking in the kitchen. Not only that; since our parents weren't there, for a change I could eat in the kitchen instead of the dining room. Estusia and Saba fasted,[22] so Warka and I had supper by ourselves. It was warm and smelled good in the kitchen. The aluminum kettle sang as it simmered on the hot stove.

After Yom Kippur came Succoth, the Jewish Festival of Booths. Since ours was a Jewish neighbourhood, between Yom Kippur and Succoth, there was a deafening noise of hammering and sawing. In no time, countless wooden "booths" (shacks) called *succoth* with palm branch roofs were erected all over the place. Some shacks were erected on balconies. It was fun to run through the courtyards in between the shacks as through an obstacle course. The religious Jews used to have their meals in these *succoth* for eight days.

My father always came home bearing gifts.

On Succoth, he would bring us cellophane cornucopia filled with "pebbles" of sugar-coated almonds. The pebbles were irregular in shape, speckled gray, pink, yellow, and green like those one could find on the shores of lakes and rivers.

On Simchat Torah,[23] which followed Succoth, my father would bring home three paper flags, one for each of us. The flags were made of cardboard paper with printed pictures of Jewish kings and the Temple in Jerusalem. The flags had windows in the Temple, which you could open and close. When you opened them you could see brightly lit candelabras inside. There were tin golden bells on the top of the wooden handle that tinkled gaily when you shook the flag.

I loved school. From September to December, the school curriculum was devoted to Christmas. We learned Polish and French Christmas carols in singing class. In arts and crafts class, we made Christmas tree decorations: long chains made out of little pieces of straw, using cranberries as beads and to hold the pieces of straw together; little paper lanterns with multicoloured cellophane panes; three-dimensional stars out of cardboard covered with silver foil; and multitudes of white "snowballs" made out of white crepe paper.

---

22  I was still too young to fast.

23  Simchat Torah (literally, "The Rejoicing in the Torah") celebrates the giving of the Torah to Moses on Mount Sinai. The Torah, the Hebrew Bible, consists of the five books Genesis, Exodus, Leviticus, Numbers, and Deuteronomy.

While we were working away, the teacher would choose the student in the class who read best to read out of a book about the childhood of Marshal Josef Pilsudski, the head of the Polish government. Marshal Pilsudski was very brave, even as a small child. He was a good student, a good son, and a great Polish patriot.

Inspired, I made my first conquest at home. Armed with a ruler, I ran, not once, not twice, but many times, all along the long and dark corridor, hitting left and right, up and down, stabbing at all the accumulated vixens and wizards. I killed all the ghosts. I felt victorious and invincible. This corridor no longer posed any threat. I felt worthy of Pilsudski. If he could do it, so could I. Somehow I felt it prudent to keep my victory my own secret.

As Christmas approached, preparations for our school's Christmas concerts accelerated. Our school was transformed. The exercise ladders, which lined three walls of our gym, were decorated with fragrant garlands of pine. The Christmas tree stood on the raised stage in the left-hand corner, facing the rows and rows of chairs that would be occupied by parents and guests. The tree was huge, reaching all the way to the ceiling, adorned with decorations made by the students, glittering with coloured candles and tinsel.

I landed the role of an angel in the Christmas concert. We all got a pattern for a costume from our teacher, and I brought it proudly home. The teacher gave explicit instructions: the costume was supposed to be a white, one-piece dress with broad sleeves with a hole for the head. It was supposed to be worn over our dress uniforms. A long, gold vertical stripe was to be glued in the middle on the front and back. On our heads, we were to wear gold cardboard bands with a gold halo disc in the back. The teacher would supply and attach our "wings" at school. My thrifty mother was not going to spend money on new white material. She had enough remnants at home to choose from, and she chose an off-white.

At the Christmas concert, the choir girls stood in a group near the piano, all in their dress uniforms of white blouses with navy sailor collars and navy pleated skirts. The angels were in the middle. All the angels were blond, blue-eyed, in gossamer snow-white dresses. All but one, the one in the front row, right in the middle, with curly black hair and an off-white dress. Isabella and my parents assured me that I was the most beautiful angel there, but it took me a long time to forgive my mother.

It wasn't only our school that changed at Christmas time. The whole of Warsaw was also transformed. There were many ancient pine trees in Warsaw, and almost all of them were decorated with tiny lights.

Near the central railway station in Warsaw was a long vertical advertisement for "E. Wedel," one of the largest Polish chocolate factories. The name was written in script with tiny white bulbs. Bulb by bulb, the sign would gradually light up, starting with the tip of the "E," so it looked as if someone were writing it out. It would light up from top to bottom, go out for a second, and light up again. It dominated the night skyline of downtown Warsaw.

There was a competition for Christmas shop window decoration. The most elaborate was the toy window of Jabklowski Brothers department store, the only department store in Warsaw. The toy window featured fast-running electrical trains running on scale models of the Polish railway system, complete with the appropriate scenery, stations, and routes. Jabklowski Brothers were housed in an imposing six-storey building, a different department on each floor. One reached each floor in an elegant roomy elevator, operated by young men or women in wine-coloured uniforms and white gloves.

Another favourite of ours was the Singer sewing machine store, which featured an animated Santa's workshop complete with red-clad elves. Most of Santa's elves were busily at work, but some of them were fooling around.

Christmas time was also Chanukah[24] time. My mother made thin crisp potato *latkes*, pancakes that we ate with sugar. We played *dreidle*[25] with my father. There were two kinds of *dreidle* manufactured in our factory. One was circular with painted coloured ribbons or zigzag designs. When you spun them, all the individual components of the colour and design disappeared blending into one. The other kind of *dreidle* was shaped like a little block, pointed at the bottom with a little stick on top that you used to spin it round. There were two varieties of the latter *dreidle* – one had carved Polish letters, the other had Hebrew letters. The four letters, which actually spelled out an acronym of the phrase "A great miracle happened there,"[26] were interpreted for the purposes of the game as signifying "take it all," "take half," "give half," and "nothing," respectively. We used to play *dreidle* for beans or wooden matches. The game was a lot of fun, especially when my father would teasingly appear to cheat when on a losing streak.

On Sundays during the winter, we would go skating in Saski Park. Since the days were short, the skating rink was illuminated early with bright floodlights. The loudspeaker would blast Strauss waltzes.

I began my skating career with twin blade skates. They were easiest to learn to skate on. They were strapped on to my boots with two leather

---

24  The Jewish Festival of Lights.

25  A special top used by children at Chanukah.

26  The miracle was that a small quantity of consecrated oil was able to keep the lamp in the temple lit eight days.

thongs, one near the toes and one at the ankle. At first, my mother would come to supervise and watch us. She didn't skate. I had to push her. She would sit in a little metal chair that had runners under its legs. The chair glided easily on the ice. The idea behind pushing the chair was to help me get used to the slippery surface and maintain my balance.

Over the years, I graduated from twin blades to a single blade. On top at the back of the blade was a little diamond-shaped stud. It went into its mate on a little metal plate on the heel of our ankle-high laced walking boots. The blade was attached to the toe of our boots by a metal band that we clamped tight with a special key. A leather strap secured the blade at the ankle. Finally, after mastering the single blade, we graduated to figure skates. Estusia was the centre of attention at the skating rink. She had natural artistic and athletic talent.

One day, all five of us – Mother, Isabella, Saba, Estusia, and I – went to a ballet performance at the Polski Theatre. We didn't go to the live theatre often so this was a special occasion. It was a splendid theatre. Comfortable red plush seats were framed on three sides by loges and balconies.

The ballet performance featured Polish folk dancing. With the Polish love for pageantry, all the Polish provinces were represented there by colourful costumes and dances specific to their provinces. There were lively *krakowiacks*, polkas, *kujawiaks,* mazurkas, and noble and sedate polonaises played to Chopin's music, complemented by the period splendour of powdered wigs and silk, brocades and lace court costumes. It was exquisite.

After the performance, children from the audience were invited to perform an impromptu dance of their choice. Estusia went up without too much coaxing; she loved to dance. She performed a *czardash* and a solo waltz. She flew across the stage all by herself. To a standing ovation, she received the first prize: a life scholarship at the Wysocka School of Dancing. We were all very proud of her. She went to the Wysocka School from then until the war broke out.

She translated her dance skills to the skating rink, and other skaters would stop their skating to watch her. Since I couldn't compete with Estusia and her grace, I developed my skills at speed skating.

In the meantime, we acquired other skills at school. Religion and patriotism went hand-in-hand in Poland. Patriotism was expressed in religious hymns, religion in accounts of patriotic exploits. Every school day would start with communal hymn singing. Our classes were ranged in pairs, everyone with her own appointed place and own partner. If someone was away or sick, the girl behind would move up one place, like musical chairs.

The hymns' lyrics were stirring and compelling, imploring the Almighty to protect Poland from its enemies. I remember some of the titles, which were also their first lines: *Kiedy ranne wstaja zorze* (When morning dawns are rising), *Pod Twa Obrone* (Under your protection), and *Boze cos Polske* (Dear Almighty that protected Poland so many centuries).

The choir sang as one angelic female voice of some three hundred assembled students and faculty.[27] Our music teacher played accompaniment. We had better be pure of tone; our teacher had an uncanny ear, and if she heard something amiss she would stop us in mid-song, pointing an accusing finger at whomever sang the false note.

Our school placed great emphasis on excellence in all subjects, but it was also known city-wide for winning trophies in intercollegiate gymnastics tournaments and drama. Led by our drama teacher, who was also our history teacher, our school performances were famous for their originality, attention to detail, and excellence in costumes, decorations, and acting.

Gym was my favourite subject. I was a proud member on our school's competitive team. We competed in junior, intermediate, and senior leagues.

Our gym outfits were spectacular. They consisted of thin black cotton T-shirts with red piping and matching shorts. On the front was a black *W* for "Wspolpraca" on a crimson disc. We wore white gym moccasins with soft leather soles, red ankle-high socks, and wore braided headbands made from red wool to keep our hair in place.

We had gym every day. We exercised on the ladders lining three walls of the gym hall. We learned balance on low benches, which when turned upside down had narrow balancing bars to exercise on.

We jumped over leather "horses" and did somersaults over a special piece of apparatus that consisted of a series of tapering wooden frames stacked on one another, the top one having a padded leather cover. The height could be lessened or increased by removing one or two frames. We landed on a stuffed leather pad.

We also had a volleyball and basketball net. The Jewish students were excused from religion classes, so while the non-Jewish students took religion, we took full advantage of the opportunity we were given to freely use the gym equipment as long as we were quiet.

In the 1930s, the Polish Ministry of Education introduced a numerical system for all high schools across Poland. The numbers were embroidered in silver thread on a blue background for grades 9 and 10 and on a red

---

27  All our teachers were women until high school.

background for grades 11 and 12. They were in the shape of small shields and were sewn on the left sleeves of our blouses. Our school's number was 141. I was very proud to wear my emblem.

In addition to reading, writing, and arithmetic, we had a choice of one foreign language – French or German. Latin was introduced in grade 9 and Greek in grade 11. All subjects were compulsory; the only choice we had was whether to take French or German. I took French.

Winters passed quickly. Snow and slush were still on the ground when the approaching spring was heralded by the Jewish holiday of Purim, when children dress up in costumes to act out the story of Queen Esther, who in ancient times saved the Jewish people from a plot by the villain Haman to destroy them. The Purim holiday commemorates the defeat of Haman's plot and sings praises to the beautiful queen Esther. Jewish stores displayed paper masks with mustaches, beards, crowns, angels, and devils, with slits for your eyes and mouth and held on by an elastic.

In my father's factory, they would get busy making *gregers*.[28] There were two kinds of *gregers*. One had a scalloped wheel sandwiched between two flat pieces of wood with a thin plywood tongue in the middle. When you twirled the handle the tongue would hit the wheel and make noise. The other kind had a wooden hammer on a flat wooden base. If you moved your hand from left to right, the hammer would knock against the base and make a clacking noise.

Whenever the name "Haman" was read out in the synagogue during the reading of the Book of Esther, the children would make noise with their *gregers* to drown out his name.

For Purim, the Jewish bakeries displayed cream-covered cakes – round, square, log-like, all covered with mountains of cream roses in pastel colours. The custom was to deliver these cakes to your friends and relatives. Since my parents were very popular and my father in particular had a wide circle of personal and business acquaintances, the doorbell rang constantly as boxes of cakes were delivered to our door. Because our family received more than we could possibly use, to the regret of us girls, many of the cakes were sent to the needy. At least we had a say in picking which ones to keep.

As far back as I could remember, my father was the president of the Jewish Deaf Association in Warsaw, called *Spojnia*.[29] *Spojnia* was a non-

---

28  Noisemakers.

29  Togetherness.

profit, mutual aid society, which dealt with the health and welfare of its members, families, widows, and orphans. It held fundraising drives on Purim and Pesach.[30] My mother organized and helped out in bazaars and auctions and canvassed donations from private individuals and from the many stores she patronized.

For Purim, we would visit my father's parents, in their apartment over his factory in Warsaw. Wearing our masks and bearing gifts, we would knock loudly and ring the doorbell. We thought that we were pretty scary, feeling sure that they would never recognize us behind our masks. They always played along with us, pretending to be very afraid and bribing us with money to leave them alone. We kept the money but didn't go away.

My father's parents were Orthodox Jews. They were sweet and gentle people. My grandmother was small and wore a brown wig.[31] My grandfather had a long white beard and always wore a *kippa*.[32] He read Jewish newspapers and was very proud when I was able to point out the letter *alef*.[33] It was all I had learned of the Hebrew alphabet.

My grandparents used to help out my father's older brother Leo at his thread factory, which was called Globus.

Leo used to take home blank spools of thread, and my grandparents would stick on the labels. My grandfather would make glue by mixing water and flour. He had strips of paper labels with a printed globe and the name of the manufacturer, Leon Wajcblum, on them. He would take a small stack of these labels and riffle them so that the ends would separate. He would use a paintbrush dipped in glue and brush the exposed ends with one stroke. Then he would roll a spool of thread and wrap it in the label. One spool after another and, *Presto!*, all the spools were labeled. Sometimes he would let me help him, but I could never match his one-stroke, one-twirl movement. I was to use this technique in pasting handbag linings in Belgium after the war, but this was much, much later.

My father's sister Zosia and her retired husband, an accountant, lived with my grandparents. Before moving in with my grandparents, Zosia and her husband used to live in Praga, located across the river from Warsaw on the left bank of the river Vistula. They never had any children. They had a little

---

30  Passover.

31  Orthodox Jewish women wore wigs as a sign of modesty.

32  Skullcap.

33  The first letter of the Hebrew alphabet.

dog when they lived in Praga. Aunt Zosia was very sad that she had to give her pet away when they moved to live with my grandparents.

Zosia was small, like my grandmother, but was more fashion-conscious. She used to wear brown or black suits with lacy blouses. She loved the clothes that my mother wore and complained that when she bought the same things they never looked as good on her. Zosia used to visit us often, and always inquired about our bowel movements. Somehow she must have thought that regular bowel movements were essential for our health. It never failed to amuse us.

My father's sister Regina also lived in Warsaw. She was married and had one son, my cousin Jurek. Jurek was about my age, and we used to collect and exchange stamps. My uncle Leo and his wife Sala had two sons, my cousins whom we saw infrequently. My father's oldest brother David was a widower. He lived with his three grown sons, Beniek, Gidalia, and Lazar.

There was a hush-hush story about my father having another brother who became a big shot in the communist party in Russia. Since the party was illegal in Poland, he lived under an assumed name in Russia to avoid retaliation against his family in Poland. One day, there was a large international gathering of workers' unions in Warsaw, and the daily papers featured his assumed name. My grandmother went to look for him at his hotel. Apparently they came face to face, but he was too frightened to acknowledge her.

My mother's relatives also lived in Warsaw. My mother's oldest brother, Aba Jaglom, was a bachelor. The story went that he was heartbroken over the untimely death of a sweetheart and thereafter never married. There were Lova and Bertha Abramovitz, my mother's cousins, whom we loved to visit, for they were very generous and would send us home by calèche. There was my aunt and uncle Boris and Ema Lewit, who had two sons, Jerzyk and Michal.

But we were closest of all to my mother's cousins Mania, Rachelka, and Sonia. The girls' father had left many years ago for the United States, leaving them in the care of their mother. They initially lived in Pruzany but eventually moved to Warsaw. Rachelka had a master's degree in classical languages. She supported herself and her mother by tutoring Latin and Greek.

In addition to being educated, Rachelka was also very athletic. She used to ride around Warsaw on her bicycle. On visits to Pruzany when I was very young, I remember she would take me on her bike to visit the gypsy camp.

Sonia attended teachers' college and married quite young. She married Abram Huberman, who owned a slipper factory. When their two children, Dadzik and Sara, were born, they moved from their apartment on Nalewki to their beautiful, modern apartment on Zelazna. Sonia was a strikingly beautiful, tall, willowy blonde with blue eyes. Generous to a fault, according to my mother, she used to support many needy families.

Spring really arrived at the time of Easter and Passover. I remember envying the Jewish children sitting on the curb of the sidewalks and polishing their new shoes with the sleeves of their coats. Everybody seemed to get new shoes. We had shoes to match our outfits, but somehow it didn't seem so special.

My parents were busy with lists and money for the Passover charities. My grandmother in Pruzany sent big wicker baskets with eggs packed in straw and geese for roasting and making fat and cracklings.

Warsaw in the spring was fragrant with the smell of the first violets and mimosa. There were flowers everywhere – in florists' shops, on street corners, and in the outdoor markets. The markets were full of superbly decorated Easter eggs. There were real eggs, wooden eggs, and sugar eggs. There were chocolate rabbits wearing ribbons around their necks and little chicks made out of fluffs of wool, holding colourful parasols.

At home, Isabella taught us how to blow out an egg without breaking the shell by making two little holes, one at the top and one at the bottom. She showed us how to decorate them with India ink and hot wax.

For Passover, out came the beautiful china, cream-coloured with a narrow dark blue band and gold Greek key design on the rim.[34] We ate *matzoh*[35] for the whole week.

My father presided over the *seder.*[36] There was great excitement over "hiding" the *afikoman*, the middle matzoh, which my father had to ransom from the children in order to continue with the ceremony.

Once a year, we three children had our father at our mercy and he had to give in to our extravagant demands. My father always entered into the spirit of the occasion and played along with us. Somehow, the past and present blended together in the real celebration of the freedom of the Jews from slavery and the welcoming of spring.

Soon after Passover came May. The first of May was International Labour Day. Warsaw celebrated it with a huge parade. All traffic was stopped along the parade route as workers from across Poland marched, each with their own flags heralding their professions. Those whose professions involved uniforms wore them.

---

34  It is the custom to use different plates and utensils for the Passover holiday.

35  Unleavened bread used at Passover to commemorate the Exodus from Egypt.

36  The ritual Passover dinner at which the story of the Exodus from Egypt is retold.

At the front of each profession and trade, four or five people proudly carried a banner that stretched across the road from sidewalk to sidewalk. After the banners came brass bands. Each group marched smartly to the beat of the big drums.

The big drums had hardly stopped pounding when they started all over again on May 3, when Poland celebrates the anniversary of the 1791 Constitution of Independence. Early in the morning, we would go to Saski Square, near the Tomb of the Unknown Soldier, to get good spots. Polish officials would make speeches, which thundered over the many loudspeakers placed in the square and along the parade route.

Then the parade would start. Each district of Poland had its own representative regiment, with a unique, identifying parade uniform. The most spectacular and popular were the Polish Ulans cavalry. They wore tall, square black hats with a gold braid, called *shakos*, double-breasted crimson tunics with rows of gold buttons, navy-blue pants with crimson piping, sheathed sabers hanging at their sides. The mounts under them trotted in disciplined step, their lustrous coats gleaming.

After them came the swashbuckling Highland regiment from the Tatry Mountains. They sported round gray hats with eagle feathers and edelweiss tucked inside their hatbands, gray capes cast rakishly off one shoulder, and carried long-handled, beautifully carved alpenstocks over their shoulders. They wore loosely knotted woolen belts, hand-woven, with red, green, and yellow geometric patterns. The ends of their belts dangled loosely, almost reaching their feet, shod with climbing boots with spiked soles. And there were many, many other colourful regiments.

Each regiment would lay a wreath at the tomb, salute, and march off, all to much applause. We waved our red and white paper flags. On the Third of May, all Warsaw was decked out in white and red flags. Everybody felt proud and patriotic.

The third of May also meant that we would start thinking more and more about the end of May, when the school year ended and summer holidays began.

When I was very young, we used to spend our summers in Pruzany. It was a small town, unsophisticated and sleepy. Pruzany had one main street and a town square where a farmers' market was held every Thursday. The town was surrounded by dense, dark forests. We never ventured there because we were told that the forest was inhabited by wolves who, when hungry, were known to attack people, especially in winter.

My grandmother's house was large. She and my grandfather had raised seven children in it. The windows had wooden shutters, which closed to form a little heart-shaped opening in the middle. The shutters were permanently closed. It was dark inside, and the light coming through the heart-shaped opening was the best way of telling whether it was day or night. The inside smelled funny, a combination of mothballs and must. My grandmother was always dressed in black taffeta dresses that rustled when she walked. She sometimes joined us for meals, but not often. She spent most of the time praying in her room. We had to walk softly and talk in whispers so as not to disturb her.

The furniture in the house was dark and massive, the beds large with soft down mattresses. When you went to sleep you sank into them and were then smothered in eiderdown blankets. There was no running water. The bedrooms had white enameled tin bowls on stands for washing up. On the wall, there was a small white water reservoir with a straight narrow pin at the bottom. When you pushed the pin in, water would come out. There was an outhouse in the yard. If you needed to go at night, there were covered porcelain chamber pots beneath the beds.

My mother used to bathe us in round wooden washtubs in the kitchen. They were made like barrels, with small staves of wood held together with metal bands. There was a wooden plug at the bottom. To empty the washtub, you put a bucket under the tub, while lifting the tub to one side and pulling out the plug. It was a two-man or two-woman operation: one held the tub, the other the plug and bucket. We always watched this operation in great anticipation, wrapped up in towels. Invariably, a rush of water would spill out of the bucket and flood the floor. We would burst out laughing, and the maids would chase us out of the kitchen. We would run away naked, losing our towels on the way. The maids would laugh to see us run for our lives.

I think that we must have been too much for my grandmother, who was getting older and was used to her own routine. So my parents had to decide what to do. My father didn't think that we had to go anywhere, but my mother wouldn't hear of it. The whole Jaglom clan gathered in Druskieniki in the summer, and my mother had her heart set on joining her family. My father protested that we couldn't possibly afford to stay in one of the resort town's expensive hotels or to rent a villa for the summer. So my mother decided that she would open a souvenir shop in Druskieniki to pay our way. My father grudgingly agreed to try it out for one year. The venture must have succeeded, because until the war we spent the rest of our summers in Druskieniki.

The bedlam started in June. We moved practically everything except the furniture and the good crystal and china. Things were packed in trunks of all sizes and in huge wicker baskets that were locked with a long steel pole stuck through two loops and secured with a heavy padlock. In addition to all our luggage, we carried baskets of food to last the five or six of us during the eight-hour train trip to Druskieniki. I couldn't wait for us to settle down and start eating. The food tasted special on the train.

But first we and our luggage took a caravan of taxis to the central train station. Once there, we had so much that we relayed the baggage by being split into pairs at intervals in the station. I would be with Warka, Estusia with Saba. While my father ran to count the luggage, my mother counted heads.

Once the train was ready to board, Warka and I were sent first to secure a Pullman compartment, which ordinarily seated eight people. We were under strict orders: I was to stretch across four seats, and Warka was supposed to block the door to stop anyone else from getting in until the baggage was disposed of and the rest of the family were safely inside. Once inside the compartment, there was more head counting, checking of baggage tickets, rearranging of luggage, all to the sounds of *Where is this?* and *Where is that?*

Nothing was lost, thank heaven! Then the whistles outside, the final *All aboard!*, and we were on our way. We went past Bialystok, past Grodno, north to Druskieniki, which was located on the northeastern tip of Poland, just south of Wilno[37] on the river Niemen, which was the natural border between Poland and Lithuania.

Druskieniki was a fashionable resort town surrounded by ancient forests of dense fir and oak. There were sulfur springs and baths where people used to come to "take the cure." The sulfurous water was reputed to have miraculous curative properties for stomach ailments, arthritis, rheumatism, rejuvenation, anything at all. Vacationers came in droves, and there were many hotels, cottages for rent, and stores to cater to their needs and wishes.

My parents rented a store with living quarters behind it on number 1 Mickiewicza[38] Street, just off the main gate of Druskieniki's one and only park.

Our store was the middle one of three stores located in a small, one-storey wooden structure. No matter how many times we came there, on the first day, it smelled as if it had been newly built, with a strong odour of fresh pine and tar. The building was constructed on a corner of a large estate belonging to a wealthy Polish widow who lived by herself in a huge mansion. She was considered aloof but was friendly to us when we occasionally met her. She sometimes wandered about her huge orchard, which contained every conceivable kind of fruit tree and berry bush. We

---

37  Vilnius. Now in Lithuania, at the time, it was part of Poland.

38  Named after Adam Mickiewicza, the Polish writer.

had permission to roam around, but we were warned by our parents not to abuse the privilege. The widow considered us well brought up and polite, and, as a result, my mother had permission at the end of the summer to take all the fruit she wanted to make preserves.

Druskieniki was blessed by nature, it was a veritable treasure trove, and we used to take full advantage of it. The trees in the forest were so tall and grew so densely that the canopy hardly admitted any of the sun's rays. It was always moist underfoot, and we walked on a thick carpet of moss, pine needles, and luscious ferns. When you walked for a while, the surface used to shine the soles of your shoes, and we used to compare whose shoes shone the most.

We would pick wild strawberries and blueberries, equipped with small wicker baskets, our arms through their handles. No matter how much we ate, there was plenty left to bring basketsful home.

After it rained, we used to pick mushrooms. At first, Warka came with us, but with time we developed our own expertise. We loved the yellow chanterelles that my mother sautéed in butter and served with a sour cream sauce. There were slippery jacks, puffballs, and a variety of others used in soups and sauces, but the real finds were the *Steinpilz*.[39] They had large brown heads and thick white stems. You really had to look for them, for they used to "hide" under moss, nestled against tree trunks. But we knew that where there was one, there were bound to be more. We strung them into long garlands, and together with garlands of strung carrots and parsnips they were left to dry in the sun and fresh air, to be used in cooking during the winter. We used the dried carrots and parsnips for soups.

These were enchanted forests, full of forest noises and small creatures running and jumping through the woods. There were furtive black moles. We used to wait very quietly to track a mole to its hole. We looked around for the other exit, for we knew that the moles dug connecting tunnels underground. Sometimes we found them. There were hares, frozen still, with only their eyes darting from side to side. When we moved, the hares would jump and disappear, their brown fur blending with the ground, perfectly camouflaged. There were squirrels galore, their reddish fur like flashes of lightning.

There were many birds in the woods. You could hear the rhythmic knocking of the woodpeckers and the *cuckoo* of the cuckoo birds. We used to count the cuckoo calls, attributing magical properties to the number

---

39  These are called "*Boletus eduli*" in Latin.

of calls. And the scent, a mixture of moisture, overripe berries, mushrooms, pine needles, and moss, was overpowering and intoxicating.

We used to pick berries and mushrooms early in the morning and eat them for breakfast. After breakfast, we went either to the public library to get books, or swimming.

The beach was on an island in the river Niemen that you reached by a long wooden pedestrian bridge. There was a ticket booth just before the bridge and changing tents on the island. The swimming area was cordoned off by a thick rope.

I learned to swim the hard way. Estusia carried me on her back all the way out to the rope and left me there. The river was broad with a swift current. I stayed by the rope as long as I could, finally kicking my legs and splashing like mad. I dog-paddled to the shore. The first time, it was scary, but eventually battling my way to the rope and back became another of my private conquests. I didn't need Estusia any more and told her so. I don't know which of us was happier.

Sometimes I went with my mother to Kaskadowki.[40] This was another invention to harness nature to the service of Man in the pursuit of youth and immortality. The northern mountains fed many streams that cascaded down and flowed into the Niemen. Their currents were swift and the water icy-cold.

Built across one tributary at Kaskadowki were two wooden structures that looked like covered bridges. One was for men, the other for women. As you entered the women's building, there was a wooden platform with a bench to sit on. Above the wooden bench were pegs for your clothes. The structure was set into the water, with an opening upstream to let the water flow in. There were narrow windows at the top to let in light.

The women would undress completely and, naked, would go down the wooden steps into the water. There they would hold onto the rope that extended around three walls. The wall opposite the platform trapped the water, forming strong, foaming little cascades: hence the name "Kaskadowki" – little cascades.

Holding the rope, the women would stand under the cascades of water beating mercilessly down upon them. The pounding water was supposed to firm flesh and reduce bulges. I used to be terrified, convinced that the cascading water would drag me down and sweep me away off to the Niemen, where I would drown and nobody would find me. At the same

---

40  Literally, "little cascades."

time, I would laugh at the shrieks of the others, and at their various shapes and bulges, praying that I would never develop the likes of them!

After lunch, from 1 to 3 p.m. was siesta time. All stores closed, and people rested. "Park time" was at three. The park was large, situated at the edge of the forest, and was very formal, with flower arrangements, manicured lawns, and stately trees. Gravel pathways led to many benches. There was a "curative" fountain where sulfurous water was piped in from a natural spring. There were twin cups suspended on chains in the fountain. You could drink from them or use them to pour water into your own cup. We were supposed to drink at least one cup a day. It was reputed to be good for you. It tasted like liquid rotten eggs.

Every afternoon in the park, Mr. Beczulka[41] conducted a military orchestra in the band shell. The performance consisted of marches and Polish folk songs, waltzes, and the like. Small children were always standing in front of the band shell, "helping" to conduct with small sticks in their hands. The audience sat on steel chairs in front of the band shell.

The park was surrounded by a tall fence, which was hidden by trees and bushes. The fence was punctured by several gates. In the afternoon, the gates were monitored by guards who inspected the entrance tickets. You could either buy the tickets for a particular performance or, as we used to do, purchase season tickets.

At the entrance to the main gate stood an old man, a veritable Santa Claus, with a white beard and twinkling blue eyes behind spectacles. He wore a white apron and cap. This was Mr. Adonoff, the best ice cream maker in Druskieniki. He had a white cart with ice cream cones painted on it. Inside the cart, kept cold by pink salt crystals, were three tubs of ice cream – vanilla, chocolate, and strawberry. There were many cafés, patisseries, and elegant ice cream parlours in Druskieniki, but his ice cream was the best.

When Uncle Lova used to come by train from Warsaw, we would run to meet him at the train station. Across from our store was a flower nursery. We would greet arriving or departing guests by first going to the nursery to get some flowers. They had everything – roses, carnations, sweet peas; African daisies in yellow, pink and brown; delicate, honey-scented alyssum in pastel colours; rainbow-coloured asters; cornflowers, poppies, dahlias, hollyhocks, and many, many more fragrant and colourful varieties.

We would show the florist which flowers we wanted to be made into pretty bouquets. He put the flowers into a half cucumber to keep them fresh. The cucumber was cut across and the flower stems were stuck into

---

41  Betzuka, which was his real name, means "little barrel."

the soft part of the cucumber where the seeds grow. Thus armed with bouquets of fresh flowers, we would greet our visitors. The magic of flowers! It never failed to bring smiles to people's faces.

The luggage having been taken directly to the hotel by porters, Lova asked where the best ice cream was. So we took him straight to Mr. Adonoff. Mr. Adonoff had two granddaughters, Tamara and Wala. Tamara was Estusia's age, Wala my age. They came from Bialystok and were not Jewish. We struck up a friendship and became inseparable.

Soon another attraction was added to Mr. Beczulka's afternoon concerts – a quartet of dancers. Under the able direction and choreography of Estusia, the four of us performed in the park, under the shell.

We danced sailors' dances clad in white blouses with sailors' collars, flared navy long pants, and sailor caps, and Polish folk dances wearing colourful Polish native costumes. Since Isabella wasn't there,[42] our mother, together with Tamara and Wala's mother, sewed our folk costumes – red satin skirts with ribbons on them, white organza blouses with puffy sleeves with elastic at the wrists and the neck. We wore flowered wreaths with colourful ribbons on our heads and rows and rows of multicoloured glass beads, which looked like miniature Christmas tree ornaments. Needless to say, we were a great success.

Too soon the summer neared its end. The time to cook our preserves was upon us. I was delegated to borrow big copper kettles from one of the hotels. My mother made the preserves, jars and jars of them – strawberries, cranberries with pears, gooseberries, and currants. She also made raspberry syrup. My father made cherry brandy from the chokecherries.

The bedlam of moving in reverse, back to Warsaw, started. But this time Warka and Father would go first, loaded with all the heavy stuff, to the background accompaniment of my mother's constant admonitions to be careful with the preserves.

Finally, there were the last goodbyes, the tearful parting from Tamara and Wala. We swore to be faithful to our friendship and never to have any other friends. The promise was forgotten with the first whistle, with the first clang of the moving train's wheels as we began our way home. Much as we loved our enchanted summers, we couldn't wait to get back home.

The trip back a blur, we arrived in Warsaw. The familiar "Wedel" sign winked its welcome. The hustle and bustle hit you immediately – newspaper boys shouting out headlines; the clang of the streetcars' warning

---

42 I don't know why she didn't come. It may have been because we didn't need a nanny in Druskieniki.

bells, and the peculiar grating sound they made as they rounded the street corners, metal grinding on metal, spewing showers of sparks. There was the sound of hawkers and peddlers shouting their wares. One I could never understand but looked forward to hearing: *Tomatoes! Tomatoes like strawberries! Strawberries! Strawberries like tomatoes!*

Our arrival back from Druskieniki would signal our return to school and our trip to the stationery store. We would get our schoolbooks at the bookstore. There wasn't much to choose from at the bookstore, since we had our list of required books, but the trip to the stationery store was different.

We had to choose wrapping paper, to protect our books and copybooks. The idea was that first you put on a book cover. Over the book cover went a thin, transparent sheet of parchment. When you gave the book or copybook to your teacher, you took off the parchment so that it would look neat and clean. The book covers came in all colours, but we chose black. Then we chose the labels. There were plain white labels; plain white with scalloped borders; white labels with black, blue, or red borders, with single, double, or triple borders. Once we got them, we couldn't return them, so we would lick them and try them on for looks on the back of our hands. The store also sold crayons, pencils, inks, India inks, glue, erasers, and pen nibs. There were many varieties of nibs: for thin script, for medium script, for calligraphy, for cartography. Then we would go home, wrap our books, and label them. We were ready for school.

The year 1937 was a very important, very serious one. I was getting ready for my exams to enter the Gymnasium.[43] Saba was getting ready for her matriculation.[44]

My parents decided that Saba needed a tutor. Thus Mieczyslaw Zielinski came into our lives. Tall, dark, handsome, and suave, he was a law student at Warsaw University. Mietek, as we grew to call him, supported himself by tutoring for meals and small gratuities. Ostensibly hired to tutor Saba, in no time he became the family's legal advisor, and the intermediary between our family and school. In addition to tutoring all three of us, Mietek also attended PTA meetings, fought our battles against unjust marks, and entertained us at suppertime.

In short, Mietek became an integral part of our family, and got involved not only in our external affairs but also in our internal squabbles. All of a

---

43  The Polish school system used to consist of four grades of grammar school, six grades of high school or Gymnasium, and two years of Lyceum. Somewhere around this time, the system changed to six years of grammar school, four years of Gymnasium, and two years of Lyceum. During this transition period, I was to enter high school.

44  Graduation from high school.

sudden Saba was no longer always right. Mietek added a new colour and dimension to our lives. All the womenfolk promptly fell in love with him. He used to tease Isabella mercilessly, treating her with exaggerated charm and courtesy. She could see through his teasing but didn't mind. The only one impervious to his charm was my mother, who used to make comments to remind him of his station in life – in her view, a tutor had little social status.

As the frantic school year neared its end, the tension, the nail biting, the dread, all gave way to enormous relief. Saba graduated, and I was promoted. But the celebration focused more on Saba than me. She had reached a milestone. Matriculation from high school was considered an important event, while promotion to high school was merely expected.

Nevertheless, Mietek made a big fuss about my making it to high school, which made me his slave for the rest of our lives. Then the inevitable happened. Saba no longer needed a tutor, but a romance had begun. She and Mietek had fallen in love. Everybody but my mother was pleased. Mietek stayed on.

The New Year of 1938 came and went.

The supper talks now centred on politics. In March, Germany entered Austria. In September, Poland's ally, Britain, signed the Munich agreement with Hitler. Neville Chamberlain declared it meant "peace in our time" and "peace with honour."

It meant neither. On October 1, 1938, German troops occupied the Czech Sudetenland.[45] On March 15, 1939, Germany occupied Prague and the rest of Czechoslovakia. Father and Mietek discussed the implications for Poland. Mietek felt that an attack on Poland was imminent, while Father belittled the significance of events, saying they were just propaganda.

In school, we each knit socks for the soldiers, using a technique that required four knitting needles. I could never get the knack of it so, as usual, Isabella came to the rescue, finishing the projects for me. We also made gas masks at school, gray wool pads that you put over your nose and mouth, held on with an elastic around your head. They had sausage-like seams that we stuffed with powdered charcoal.

---

45 A border region of Czechoslovakia that takes its name from the Sudetes mountains, which today run along the border of Czechoslovakia and Poland. Before 1945, more than three million Germans lived in this area, which had been a traditional part of Bohemia. Many Germans in the Sudetenland became supporters of the Nazis. The Sudetenland was ceded to Germany as a result of the infamous Munich Pact in 1938, signed by Germany, the United Kingdom, France, and Italy. (Czechoslovakia was not invited to the talks.) The Sudetenland was returned to Czechoslovakia after World War II. The Sudetenland's German population was expelled to Germany following its return to Czechoslovakia.

With the German occupation of Czechoslovakia, talk of war intensified. Poland began mobilizing in July and August. In Druskieniki, all the vacationers left in a hurry, by train, cars, carts, whatever.

My father came from Warsaw to urge my mother to pack up and leave. Nothing doing. It was preserve-making time and my mother was making preserves. While the whole world around us was leaving in a panic, my mother was making preserves.

I was sent off to get the copper kettles, and, on the way home through the back alleys that ran parallel to the main street, I added to the excitement by banging the kettles like marching drums. I could see people's startled faces when they discovered the source of the drumming. Finally, we caught one of the last trains still running on schedule and arrived home.

In Warsaw, loudspeakers blared patriotic songs in between announcements urging all the men to report to their mobilization stations. Posters featuring the face of a smiling Marshal Smigly-Rydz[46] appeared everywhere. Detachments of men and boys dug trenches in the parks.

Saba, by then working in an export–import business, brought home sacks of rice and flour. My father brought home boxes and boxes of sardines and chocolate. Mietek joined the army.

War broke out on September 1, 1939.

The cellars in our building, normally used for storing potatoes and coal for the winter, were transformed into bomb shelters. The air over Warsaw was pierced with shrill sirens announcing air raids. We would grab our prepared bundles of food and water and run down to the shelters. There we would join our neighbours. We finally got to know the people next to whom we had lived all our lives and whom we had never met before. We found out that our next-door neighbours were the Fogel family, consisting of Mr. and Mrs. Fogel and their daughter Chaya, who attended an all-girls Jewish high school called *Yehudia*.[47]

We struck up a friendship with Chaya, who was amazed at our ignorance of Jewish subjects. We in turn were amazed at her lack of knowledge of greater Warsaw. Chaya's life kept her very much within the narrow confines of the Jewish part of Warsaw.

One Friday night, during a lull in the bombardment, I went to visit our neighbours. Mrs. Fogel opened the door. It was dark inside, so I switched on the light. Mrs. Fogel started screaming and I ran back to our apartment, crying.

---

46 One of the leading personalities of the "government of colonels" established upon the death (in 1935) of Marshall Pilsudski.

47 *Yehudia* is the Hebrew word for a female Jew.

I couldn't comprehend what was going on. I was sure that I was going to be punished for doing something awful. My father asked me what had happened, and, when I told him, he started laughing. He told me that because it was considered work, orthodox Jewish families like the Fogels did not turn the lights on or off on the Jewish Sabbath,[48] the day of rest.

My father asked me to come with him to the Fogels, but I refused. I was mortified and terrified. So my father went next door and brought Mr. Fogel back with him. They sat at the dining room table as my father explained to Mr. Fogel what had happened. Mr. Fogel smiled and explained that his wife was startled and hadn't meant to scream at me. I stood next to my father, his arm around me, not quite sure if I could trust Mr. Fogel.

Then my father and Mr. Fogel became embroiled in a discussion about rituals and the spirit of Judaism. My father supported his arguments by quoting chapter and verse by heart from the Bible. Mr. Fogel disputed the accuracy of my father's quotes. Father brought a big Bible to the table and proved his point to Mr. Fogel. Mr. Fogel was flabbergasted to discover that my father knew the Bible by heart. I was amazed, both at my father's knowledge and the fact that I had never heard him discuss or practice our religion. My father and Mr. Fogel met a few times and continued their discussions in the bomb shelter.

In the air-raid shelters, we would sit and listen to the noises outside. "Experts" would identify the sounds of planes as "ours" and "theirs." Small children wailed as their mothers tried to comfort them. We listened to the hiss of the incendiaries raining down on Warsaw. When we heard the terrifying scream of a falling bomb, we held our breath until we heard the explosion, breathing out when we knew that it hadn't fallen on our heads. We went back up when we heard the long wail of the *all clear* sirens.

We would wash to try to get rid of the coal dust that clung to our clothes and skins and got into our hair. One day, my mother was watering the plants when the sirens started again. Everybody went down, my mother and I the last to go. When we were half-way down the stairs, there was a tremendous explosion. The whole house shook, and I heard the rumble of an avalanche of stones. I grabbed my mother, and we continued down and made it to the shelter. My father stood at its entrance, pale as a sheet.

At the *all clear*, we went back up. There was broken glass and torn plaster all over the front of our apartment, and a big hole in the wall where

---

48  This is the strict interpretation of keeping the Sabbath as a day of rest when no work is to be done, even so much as turning the lights on or off. The Jewish Sabbath runs from sundown Friday to sundown Saturday.

our balcony used to be. The floor of our third-floor balcony, made of a solid sheet of iron, was now resting on the balcony of the first floor. It had sliced through the second-floor balcony.

The building across the street had all but disappeared. It had caved in, collapsed as if it had been a dollhouse. Only the sides were still standing. Exposed to the world were the private remnants of people's homes – the wallpaper on the walls, the bathtubs and toilets still anchored to the tiled floors. We stood there, numb, thanking God that we escaped harm.

The bombing of Warsaw went on and on and then suddenly stopped. We were nervous about the silence, expecting the air-raid siren. But nothing happened. By this time, we had no water and no electricity.

One day, Isabella came running to tell us that a pickle factory was on fire and that we should go and get pickles. My mother objected, but Isabella said that nothing could be done about the pickles anyway. I ran out with Isabella.

We ran through unfamiliar streets, through ruins where houses used to stand. We passed a dead horse lying in a puddle of blood in the middle of the street.

At the still-burning pickle factory, people were running around trying to grab the big square tins of pickles, still scorching to the touch. There were ruptured cans all over the place, streams of pickle juice under our feet. People were going crazy. We joined the frenzy, pushing and kicking until each of us got hold of an intact can of pickles, which we brought back home huffing and puffing. I didn't even like pickles.

My father boarded up the gaping hole where our balcony used to be. My mother and Isabella cleaned up the dining room. The crystal goblets and most of the crystal glasses had been shattered, the buffets heavily damaged.

The living room/dining room was now cast in perpetual gloom. Boards over the hole in the wall where the balcony had been blocked the light. It was drafty and cold. We spent most of our time either in the kitchen or in our room.

One day, my mother went to work on the living room. She removed a tile from the big fireplace, put a small wood stove in front of the fireplace, and attached a long curved tin pipe from the stove through the hole where the tile was removed, thus using the fireplace as the stove's chimney. Since there was no coal, she stocked the wood stove with carved chess pieces. My father had brought them back from his factory by the sackful. The chess pieces burned well and kept the room warm.

At first, we used candles for light, then kerosene lamps, the glass of which had to be continually cleaned, since it would get blackened from the smoke. Eventually, carbide lamps appeared on the market. These became so popular that everybody started to manufacture them. The lamps were made by fitting two cans into each other, one a little larger than the other. The top can was filled with carbide, the bottom with water. A little funnel with a burner head was soldered on top of the carbide can.

The carbide looked like small green rocks. When mixed with water, it produced a noxious gas, but when the mixture was lit, the odour would disappear. The flame was as bright as an electric bulb. We used these lamps to light the dining room table and the kitchen. We used candles in the bedrooms.

Isabella and I would get water from a nearby park where people queued in front of a pump. One day, I got bored waiting in the line. I left Isabella and wandered off onto a nearby hill. From there, I had a good view of the park below me.

There were stacks and stacks of rifles on the meadow, muzzles in the air, the barrels supporting one another, like so many haystacks in the field. They were the rifles that the Polish soldiers had surrendered to the Germans. They were guarded by soldiers from a German field kitchen, the gray German uniforms[49] surrounding a covered truck with a chimney from which a puff of white smoke escaped.

The scene was calm and peaceful. Before long, a young German soldier joined me on the hill. He had a loaf of pumpernickel bread in one hand and a knife in the other. He smiled at me, cut a large piece of bread and extended it to me. I knew my duty. I looked at him with contempt, turned my back on him, and went down to join Isabella. I was not about to accept a gift from an enemy. Isabella was watching this scene from below and berated me for being stupid. Sure enough, a swarm of children surrounded the soldier, begging for the bread.

I wasn't really hungry. My mother had been baking bread every day since the beginning of the war, but I hadn't seen pumpernickel bread since the war started.

Food was hard to get. Farmers came to town with carts loaded with fruits, vegetables, eggs, butter, and cheese. But they would not accept any paper money, only coins.[50] They accepted Polish coins but preferred German pfennigs. The electricity was reconnected in some places, and by word of mouth people learned that some bakeries were back in operation. Once or twice a week, we stood in line to get some bread.

---

49  These were regular German army (*Wehrmacht*) troops.

50  I think they reasoned that even if the paper became worthless, coins would still be worth something because of the metal content.

My mother embroidered the word *Taubstummer*[51] in black gothic letters on a yellow armband for my father. Carrying a wooden tray in front of him supported by a leather belt around his neck, my father ventured forth to the cafés and patisseries patronized by the German soldiers. He sold hand-painted postcards made of very thin plywood, featuring cartoons and funny pictures. These cards, made in his factory, were leftovers from World War I. Soon pumpernickel bread appeared on our table again, along with dairy products and fruits and vegetables.

Saba finally got word that Mietek was all right, but in hiding. Mietek risked his life to come and visit us. He wanted to escape to eastern Poland, which in November 1939 was occupied by Russia. He implored my parents to leave everything and come east with him. My mother wouldn't hear of it. She said that she had survived one war and that she would survive another, that hard as it was during the war, it would be even harder after the war. As an officer, Mietek had to run away, but we had nothing to fear.

A terrible few days followed. Despite her strenuous objections, my mother finally gave in to Saba's pleading. She helped Saba pack a knapsack with warm clothing, a bit of money, and a little food, and, following tearful goodbyes, Saba left with Mietek.[52]

My mother was inconsolable for days. Though Saba promised that she would write and keep in touch, my mother was in mourning for her, convinced that she would never see her again. She was right.

An uneasy calm followed. Warka got married and left us. My father resumed his work at the factory with a greatly reduced workforce. Estusia and I returned to school briefly. One day, we were called to the office of our principal, who, with tears in her eyes, told us that we could no longer come to school; Jews were not allowed to attend non-Jewish schools. She was very upset. She also told us that she was not sure if her school would remain open for long.

At first, we were not too upset. But my parents were, especially my father. One day, he came home a changed man. His hair had turned all white. His face was composed but his eyes were tortured, full of tears that he had to wipe away with his handkerchief. In his hand, he had a piece of paper: a receipt for our factory. The Germans had confiscated his factory.

On that day, the nightmare began.

---

51  "Deaf and Dumb."

52  Sabina and Mietek survived the war and made a new life for themselves in Sweden.

# The Warsaw Ghetto[1]

What is literature? What is a word? It is funny, but in my opinion one can compare a word to the moon. For what is the moon but a dead planet, having no light of its own, only reflecting the sunlight? Who could have guessed, looking at the cold image of the moon, that it borrows its radiance from the hot, blinding sun? And a word? Isn't it only a reflection of a deed? And can a word faithfully represent a deed? No, never. That is why I know in advance that whatever I shall write will be just a collection of words, understood only by those who saw and survived.

Nobody will be able to give the world a faithful account of what was happening in this corner of crime and barbarism. Perhaps the orbit surrounding human imagination is infinite, but this lies even further, beyond human comprehension.

The year 1939 was the first year of meeting the threat of the war, of the victims that the war insatiably claimed and the first contact with the bloody tentacles of fascism.

Soon, after a few days of seeing the green uniforms[2] on the streets, one could *feel* their presence. More often and louder, newspapers reported the

---

1  This chapter consists of diary material written in Corbion, Belgium, in June 1945.

2  Most likely *SS Ordnungspolizei* ("*ORPO,*" literally, "order police"). The SS (or *Schutzstaffel*) was formed as Hitler's elite bodyguard, but later was given vast "police" intelligence and military powers. By the late 1930s, Heinrich Himmler, the head of the SS, had created a huge police-state apparatus, The SS was given the primary responsibility for the so-called "Final Solution" of the Jewish "problem," which caused the murder of six million Jews. The SS had two main organizational divisions. The *Allgemeine-SS* (literally, "general SS") and the *Waffen-SS* (literally, "armed SS"). The main subdivision of the *Allgemeine-SS* was the *Reichssicherheitshauptamt* ("*RHSA,*" literally, "Reich Security Central Office") The *RHSA* was in turn subdivided into the *Ordnungspolizei,* and the *Sicherheitspolizei* (literally, "security police"). The *Sicherheitspolizei* was in turn made up of the *Gestapo* (*Geheime Staatspolizei,* literally, "secret police") and the *Kriminalpolizei* (*KRIPO,* literally, "criminal police"). The *RHSA*

mysterious disappearance of individuals who left their homes, never to return. There were no clues whatsoever to their whereabouts. At first, it was strange and incomprehensible, but soon it was all too clear who were the perpetrators of these mysterious disappearances, and we painfully experienced the boot of fascism on our own skins.

The atmosphere in town[3] was soaked with fear, chilling the blood in our veins. One could not be sure of a moment or a day. Degenerates, like hyenas in search of prey, cruised the streets, terrorizing the defenceless population. The anti-Semitic propaganda had left its mark. Bands of Polish children, seven years old and up, ran through the streets, armed with sticks, screaming anti-Semitic slogans and beating every Jew they encountered.

We hear so much about Polish patriotism, their heroism, their hatred of conquerors and enemies. How then can we explain their collaboration with the Germans in this war? Many of their children walked the streets with the Germans, pointing out Jews, some of their women spent their time with the Germans in night clubs, cabarets, and cafés. Never mind their men, whose very existence depended on supporting the German interests. Indeed, the Germans received a welcome in Poland, beyond their wildest dreams.

It is not surprising that, having received such support, German sadists flourished unhindered.

One day, a Jew was caught on the street. He was taken to clean toilets in German apartments. He was treated politely, asked about his family, his life, and his circumstances. When they heard that his life was hard, they offered him a well-paying job and commiserated about the hardships of war.

In the end, he was offered cake and beer. At first, he refused, but he was forced to accept. He started to eat and drink. As he put the bottle to his mouth, one of the scoundrels smashed the bottle with all his might down into the unfortunate's mouth. The bottle stuck and broke in his throat. Then they took him and threw him onto the street. Passers-by took pity on him and took him to a nearby emergency hospital where, after a few hours of agony, he died.

---

also included the *Sicherheitsdienst* (*SD*, literally, "security service," which looked after intelligence – foreign and domestic and espionage). The *Waffen-SS* had two main subdivisions: the *Totenkopfverbande* (literally, "death's head battalions"), which ran the concentration and extermination camps; and the *Verfugungstruppen* (literally, "disposition troops), which served as elite combat battalions alongside the regular army (*Wehrmacht*) troops. Another SS group, the *Leibstandarte* (Hitler's bodyguards), did not fit into the conventional SS command structure. Though nominally subordinate to Himmler, they were not, in effect, controlled by Himmler as they had sworn personal loyalty to Hitler.

3 Warsaw.

The Germans were issuing new decrees against Jews all the time. At first, Jews were given thirty minutes to evacuate a designated street. Within half an hour, accompanied by screams and blows from the Germans, the Jews were to pack only their personal necessities and move out of their homes. They did not know where they were moving. Curfew was at 9 p.m. Anyone caught on the street after 9 p.m. was exposed to untold dangers. Resettlements took place shortly before sunset.

The next decree ordered all Jews ten years old and over to wear a white band with a blue Star of David on their right arms. Not wearing the armband was punishable by death.

The Germans often resorted to the following trick. They would stroll about in twos or threes. When a Jew walked by them, the German in front would rip off the Jew's armband and signal his comrades. Not wearing an armband! Obviously his friends now had a legitimate reason – in the best case to beat the victim, in the worst case to shoot him dead.

Sensing what would come, my father had already taken whatever he could out of the factory, such as finished products and leather transmission belts from the machines. He stored it all in the cellar of our apartment building, where we ordinarily stored coal and potatoes for the winter.

He transformed our bathroom into a storage place, building shelves from floor to ceiling. It was jammed, packed with the products from his factory: hand-carved chess pieces, chess boxes, painted and carved picture frames, pens with tiny animals carved on top of them, and many more items.

The Germans used "laws" to facilitate their pillage and robbery. They issued a decree that ordered the Jews to surrender all their valuables, furs, and businesses. My mother and I went to our designated depot and handed in her furs. The fur collars were ripped off our coats. My father's factory was requisitioned by the Germans. They came one day, sealed the factory, and gave my father a receipt, telling him that after the war he would get it back.

The Germans conducted apartment searches to make sure that the Jews complied with the decrees. One day, there was a knock at our door – a young SS[4] officer and two privates.

My mother and I were at home. The officer told us that they had come to inspect our apartment. They wiped their feet before entering. The officer came into our living room, looked around, and told his soldiers to search the whole apartment. He told my mother and me to stand in front of him. He body-searched us, moving his hands over our bodies and under our

---

4 *Schutzstaffel.*

clothes. The soldiers came back carrying my stamp collection, which my father had started when he was still a little boy and which he gave me on my tenth birthday. That is all they took. Polite throughout, they left, thanking us for our co-operation. My mother wept, partly from fear, partly from relief that nothing worse had happened.

Thus, the days passed in continuous worry and uncertainty. All kinds of rumours circulated. Here and there started the construction of brick walls, three metres high.

What did it mean? Some said that they were barricades for the forthcoming war with Russia, others said they were something else. Wherever one went, the word "walls" was on everybody's tongue. Walls, walls, red brick walls with barbed wire and broken glass on top like spectres of future gloom, looming over everyone's head. Black clouds gathered over the Jewish population. Everybody knew, but nobody dared to say it aloud – these were the borders of the future ghetto.

Ten gates manned by German gendarmes and Polish and Jewish police linked the ghetto to the outside world. Ten gates, witnessing thousands and thousands of human tragedies, witnessing the fighting at their steps for the right to live. People's survival depended on whether there was a good or a bad gendarme on guard at the gate.

And if a good one, on the other side were the Polish kids waiting to attack us and rob us. Poor Jewish families, having no other means of support, became smugglers. At the risk of losing their lives, they forced their way through to the Aryan side, bought victuals, and brought them back to be resold at much higher prices. And thus they survived.

Many did not return from such trips; their blood coloured the cobblestones red. But the shootings did not frighten others who followed. They had no choice: It was more frightening to die of hunger than from a bullet. Would that the human mind were endowed with the ability to predict the future and the events that were to come in but a few months! All of us would have chosen to finish it right there and then, rather than day after day to suffer, to despair, to lose our health, and then finally to be annihilated in the German crematoria.

The ghetto population grew, swelled by the daily transports of Jews from neighbouring towns and hamlets. It became worse and more overcrowded each day. Hunger was rampant, there was an epidemic of typhus. Bodies bloated from hunger lined the streets.

Driven to despair, hungry people attacked pedestrians, grabbing purses and parcels. But this was only one side of the coin. On the other side were the nouveau-riche elite. The shop windows displayed southern fruits,

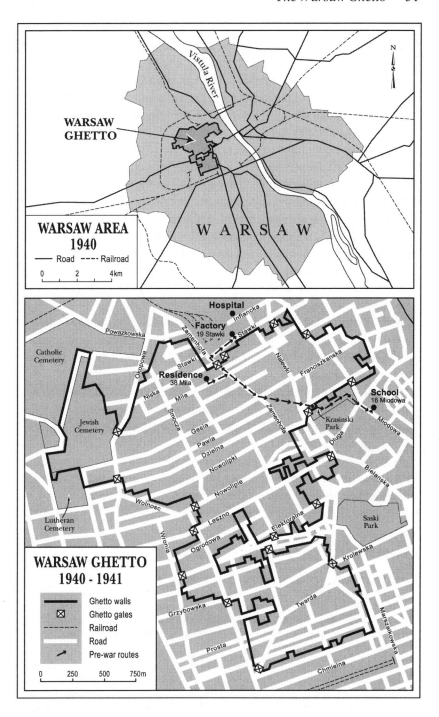

WARSAW
GHETTO

**WARSAW AREA
1940**

—— Road  ---- Railroad

0      2      4km

N

Vistula River

W  A  R  S  A  W

Hospital
Inflancka
Factory
19 Stawki    Stawki
Powazkowska
Zamenhofa
Nalewki
Franciszkanska
Catholic
Cemetery
Okopowa
Stawki
Residence
38 Mila
Niska
Mila
Zamenhofa
School
16 Miodowa
Miodowa
Jewish
Cemetery
Smocza
Gesia
Krasinski
Park
Dluga
Pawia
Bielanska
Dzielna
Nowolipki
Wolnosc
Nowolipie
Saski
Park
Lutheran
Cemetery
Leszno
Elektoralna
Wronia
Ogrodowa
Krolewska

**WARSAW GHETTO
1940 - 1941**

━━━ Ghetto walls
⊠ Ghetto gates
---- Railroad
━━━ Road
↗ Pre-war routes

0    250    500    750m

Grzybowska
Twarda
Marszalkowska
Prosta
Chmielna

delicatessen kinds of foods and cakes, shop windows beneath which the hungry swallowed their saliva; the hungry, falling from exhaustion, whose last sight was of the marvels forever out of their reach.

One could hear music from the cafés, restaurants, and cabarets, and the singing and laughter of the patrons. As they left, laughing and drunk, tens of trembling frozen arms stretched out to them for alms, toward the light and warmth of a momentarily opened door.

But the poor could not enjoy the light and warmth for long. Screams and canes chased them away. Who cared that they were frozen and hungry? Who cared that hundreds died on the streets? To the eager lackeys, it was more important to make sure that no lice got on the elegant dress of the lady and no dust on the shiny patent leather shoes of the gentleman.

And when the hungry on the streets grew in numbers from day to day, and their frozen wounds called out for revenge from heaven, and the papers they used to cover themselves were scattered, exposing their emaciated, naked bodies, it was said, *They are clowns, exposing their bodies to extort more alms from people.*

And when exhausted by frost and hunger, pushed by necessity, driven by the wild, blind instinct of survival, the hungry attacked these soulless dolls, grabbing at the gingerly held packages under their arms, they said, *Hey, hold the bandit!*

And the Jewish Police,[5] who will forever remain a blot on the ghetto's history, beat the "bandits" mercilessly until they often fell dead under the canes. This is the way that life went on and boiled within the perimeter of the red walls.

There were two kinds of Jewish police. The ones with blue bands in their caps were the regular police. The ones with green bands were the secret police and were called "The Thirteen."[6] They were the worst and

---

5 In September 1939, the German occupiers of Warsaw ordered the creation of a *Judenrat*, a council of leading Warsaw Jews whose responsibility was to direct the affairs of the community in the interest of the occupiers. One of its agencies was a police force that, at one time, numbered some 2,000. The force, for example, rounded up citizens for forced labour and was active in the expulsion of the Jews from the Warsaw ghetto; it was loathed by the community.

6 A rival agency to the *Judenrat* sanctioned and encouraged by elements of the German occupation regime in the Warsaw ghetto. Its primary division, the "Office to Combat Usury and Profiteering in the Jewish Quarter of Warsaw," was a police force wearing a green rather than the blue identification band of the regular police. The leader, Abraham Gancwajch, was suspected of being a Nazi agent. Despite its welfare work pretensions, it was an agent of blackmail and corruption.

were alleged to collaborate with the Germans. During the *Aktions*,[7] each policeman had to deliver a quota of heads for deportation. We could hear them shouting to each other: *Hey, how many heads have you got. I got my quota. I can lend you three.*

The Germans issued a decree announcing that all Jews had to register their pianos. The Poles roamed the ghetto in search of good bargains. My father brought a Pole to our apartment and sold him our grand piano, happy that he could get a good price for it. The Pole left a deposit with my father, told him that he would give him the remainder upon receiving the piano's three legs, and then would send people to move the piano.

A rendezvous was arranged on the Aryan side of the ghetto. My father removed the piano's legs and leaned the piano against the living room wall. He gave the legs to Estusia to give to the Pole in exchange for the money. Estusia was to cross to the Aryan side via the courthouse on Leszno Street. This route was commonly used, as one side of the courthouse faced the ghetto, the other the Aryan side. At the time, the courthouse was still laxly guarded.

Estusia, loaded down with the three heavy piano legs, went on her errand. About three hours later, she returned, shaking and in tears, with no piano legs and no money.

She told us that she had delivered the legs and received the money as prearranged. But she was followed by two Poles who saw the transaction. As she approached the courthouse, they stopped her and told her that unless she gave them the money, they would denounce her as a Jewess to the Germans.

And yet among the general decay and demoralization was something that many people don't know about. Something beautiful and noble. If you listened carefully through the din and tumult of the street noises, you could hear a plaintive melody of a Hebrew song, sung by young, warm hearts.

It was my neighbour, Chaya Fogel, who decided that our Jewish education left a lot to be desired and introduced us to Hashomer Hatzair, a socialist Jewish youth group.[8] Its followers considered it the best educational organization of all the Jewish youth movements. Its opponents considered it communist.

---

7  *Aktions* (literally, "actions") consisted of the roundup of Jews for deportation to various labour or death camps.

8  Hashomer Hatzair ("The Young Guards") was a Zionist youth group in Eastern Europe. It had a distinctly socialist orientation. Its goal was to establish *kibbutzim* (collective settlements) in Palestine.

Hashomer Hatzair was organized along military lines into divisions, battalions, and platoons. My battalion's name was Hamishmeret[9] and my battalion commander was Shimon Heller. I've forgotten my platoon's name, but my platoon commander was Lilit. The division bore her name.

Estusia in 1937.

On our first meeting, I fell in love with Shimon. Shimon, ignorant of my existence, fell in love with Estusia. Estusia dropped out after a short while to pursue her nursing career, and, as far as Shimon was concerned, I only existed as Estusia's younger sister.

I decided to turn things around and became very active in the organization, at first only to try to make Shimon notice me in my own right, and then because I grew to like the organization and everything it stood for.

We all had Hebrew names in the organization. Mine was "Hagar," because, as an assimilated Jew, I was considered to have come from another "tribe."[10] I didn't know how to speak Yiddish and knew practically next to nothing about Jews and Judaism.

I learned about Palestine, about the Zionist movement, the hardship of the Jewish pioneers in Palestine, and the Arab opposition. I learned about compassion for the less fortunate.

I soaked up my new education like a sponge. I loved and sang all the Hebrew songs, whose lyrics I didn't understand, but whose melody spoke to my heart. I remember Shimon telling us that, later in life, we would probably forget the ideology, but we would never forget the melodies and words of the songs. He proved to be prophetic.

I learned about life and death, and in particular about the value of life, and the value of death. We used to conduct mock trials based on books. One in particular, by Rabindranath Tagore,[11] was the story of prisoners awaiting their death sentences together in a cell. Each of us picked a character. We also picked people to act as the judge, the prosecutor, the

---

9 The Guard Post.

10 In the Bible, Abraham's wife, Sarah permits Abraham to take a concubine because she is barren. Hagar was the concubine of Abraham. She and Abraham had a child, Ishmael, whom the Arabs consider to be the first of their people.

11 Rabindranath Tagore (1861–1941) was a Hindu poet and Nobel prizewinner.

defence counsel and the jury. We debated the merits and demerits of each character, their crimes, and their punishments. In retrospect, there is no doubt in my mind that these discussions were the seeds for the future Warsaw uprising, when the conclusion was that death by resistance was preferable to death by slaughter.

My parents knew nothing of my activities in Hashomer Hatzair. Had they known, they would have forbidden it.[12] I told them that I belonged to a social club.

The Jewish youth did not forget its obligations in these worst of times. Conditions were worse than hard. But no one was discouraged. We had meetings in private apartments, each time somewhere else. Quietly hummed Hebrew songs penetrated the depths of our hearts, setting them beating to a common rhythm. It is hard to imagine the great power of such songs. They fired the flames in our young, hot hearts, welding us together.

During the hours we spent together, the reality of our daily nightmare was overshadowed by the dream of sunny Israel with its palm trees and orchard groves. Our hearts swelled with hope when we learned about the progress in the construction of the *kibbutzim*[13] and the gains that had been made. We rejoiced with our comrades in Israel over the first sprouts, seeded with their own hands. How much toil it cost for these small shoots to sprout! How much sweat and blood were spilled in the process of draining the swamps and seeding the land? How many victims fell due to malaria?[14]

But these little green shoots more than compensated for it all – future bread. And our eyes filled with tears and our fists clenched when we looked on helplessly at the fire eating up this hard labour, Jewish fields going up in flames started by the Arabs.

And again our fists clenched helplessly when we saw multitudes of children and the elderly being marched toward *Umschlagplatz*.[15] Pink posters with huge screaming black letters burned our eyes. They advertised "voluntary resettlement."

The barbarians struck at the most sensitive chord of the ghetto: hunger. Everybody who volunteered for deportation would receive three kilograms

---

12 My mother in particular was very snobbish. She would not consider it proper for me to associate with what she would call "riffraff" or "common youth."

13 Collective settlements in Israel.

14 The land was swampy and infested with malaria and had to be drained before seeding could take place.

15 *Umschlagplatz* (literally "place of transshipment") was a former public school used as a collection point for deportations.

of bread and one kilogram of jam. Yes, it was too tempting to refuse. Thousands and thousands of hungry people marched to their deaths for three kilograms of bread and one kilogram of jam. And we had to watch it with eyes misting with tears and fists clenched until they hurt.

We stripped down the murderous posters in vain. These escapades often ended with the gendarmes shooting at our fleeing figures. Our begging and pleading did not help either. The Jewish businessmen were cold and unmoved. They did not believe in the "fables" about crematoria. The elite, the intelligentsia, regarded our agitating as revolutionary propaganda. But if propaganda, to what end? This they could not answer.

Then they started to deport refugees, those in orphanages and in shelters for the homeless. Here we had the first sign of heroism. Among the others were a few orphanages founded by the famous author and educator Doctor Janusz Korczak.[16] Thanks to him hundreds of Jewish orphans had clean beds, food, education, and expert psychological help.

When Doctor Korczak was first approached with the order to deport the children, he refused, but when he realized that he had no choice, he marched in front of them. He did not leave them – he perished with them. Glory and honour to him. It is such a pity that people like him were exceptions, not the rule. New decrees coloured the ghetto walls. New decrees, new traps. All those unemployed or otherwise unoccupied had so many days to present themselves voluntarily at the *Umschlagplatz*. Disobeying the order was punishable by death.

As mushrooms follow rain, new workshops of all kinds sprouted throughout the ghetto. People queued for hours in front of the shops for a job.

Those with enough money to bribe the officials were the first hired. And those waiting outside were given numbers to present themselves the following day, and the next day. On the third day came trucks bearing Germans and Ukrainians who picked people right off the street and loaded them on to the trucks. Thus ended the first massive deportation. Only those with jobs and the small number of those who succeeded in hiding remained in the ghetto.

At first, all we knew for sure was that the transports went to Treblinka. Many rumours were floating around about what was happening at Treblinka, but nothing was known for sure until one day, in an incredible

---

16  Janusz Korczak (pseudonym for Dr. Henryk Goldschmidt) was a well-known writer and educator who became involved with handicapped Jewish children. In the Warsaw ghetto, he headed an orphanage and in August 1942 voluntarily and with great dignity accompanied the children to the Treblinka death camp.

feat, one of our youth group escaped from the "work camp." He told us what was happening. Learning that Treblinka was a death camp reinforced our determination to fight the deportations.

My father obtained a permit to establish a workshop to manufacture wooden picture frames, considered an essential industry for the German Reich, and thus protecting us from deportation. He was given the use of an empty apartment for his workshop, at number 41 Mila Street, literally across the street from our apartment. My father gave Estusia the keys to 41 Mila Street and told us to carry over some wooden picture frames to make the vacant apartment look occupied.

My mother tied the bundles of frames with string, and we started making our trips to the apartment across the street.

One day, my father had gone out somewhere, my mother was alone in our apartment, and Estusia and I were on our last trip to the "workshop" apartment. Outside in the street, we heard the sounds of shrieks, whistles, shooting, and people yelling, *Raus! Raus!* [17]

*Blockade!* [18] The street was cordoned off by lines of German soldiers, accompanied by Polish and Jewish police. [19] Trucks waited on the street, German soldiers were running up and down the stairs chasing people out of the buildings into the street. Once forced out of the building, the people were made to kneel in the middle of the street.

Estusia and I were desperate. We ran down the stairs and tried to find one of the hiding places, called *Bunkiers,* which were in every building and which we were sure must also exist in this building. We found it. But as strangers, we were chased away. [20] We had no choice but to return to the empty apartment and await our fate.

We sat on the floor, behind the door, telling each other jokes to ward off the fear and desperation. The shooting, yelling, and whistling continued on the street and in the courtyard. We saw bedbugs crawling on the floor. Estusia wanted to kill them with her shoe, but I said, *Leave them be, if you kill them,* they *will kill us too!*

---

17  "Out! Out!"

18  The blockading or barricading of streets to facilitate forcible deportations to the death camps.

19  A variety of German police administrations operated in the occupied areas, including Gestapo, Security and Order; in addition, local police made up of various occupied ethnic groups operated under the German civilian and military authorities.

20  Ironically, the occupants were captured and, by refusing us entrance, we were saved from capture and deportation.

So we sat, cringing and shifting to let the bedbugs move around us. Suddenly, there was the sound of heavy boots running up the stairs, and a man's voice screaming, *Raus! Raus!*

I knew our end had come. The soldier pushed open the door with his rifle butt, swinging the unlocked door in on us. He stepped into the apartment,[21] and, seeing it empty, ran out again. He never noticed us hidden behind the door.

Hours must have passed. We sat there, holding our breaths, agonizing over what had befallen our mother, all alone in the apartment. It was deathly silent; the people had been marched away, the trucks gone.

We finally ventured out. There wasn't a soul around. We saw the doors of the cellars open, the *Bunkiers* empty. There was nobody else, just the two of us. We ran like crazy to our apartment. There was nobody on the street, nobody anywhere. We rang the bell. My mother opened the door. She was all right. Being deaf, she hadn't heard a thing.

Soon afterward, my father abandoned the idea of the picture frame workshop.[22] He registered as a woodcarver and got a job working outside the ghetto, at the German Military Cemetery.

The Germans needed a cemetery in Warsaw. Wounded German soldiers from the Eastern Front and from Stalingrad were shipped to Warsaw for treatment and rehabilitation.[23] Those who died were buried in Warsaw. Speculation in the ghetto was that all the burials meant the Germans had taken a beating at Stalingrad.

My father's job was to carve the name, rank, and dates of birth and death on the dead soldiers' crosses. As such, my father was part of a

---

21 The apartment at 41 Mila Street, designated to be my father's workshop. Events happened so quickly, it was never used. On this occasion, Estusia and I went there for the first and last time to put some wooden picture frames there to make it look occupied.

22 This must have been around July 1942 when the mass transports of Jews were taken to Treblinka. The ghetto was decimated. It was no longer possible to establish small workshops, which in the first place, were a Nazi artifice that they established only to subsequently abandon. From then on, anybody who fell victim to a *Blockade* was taken to *Umschlagplatz* and deported, mostly to their deaths at Treblinka, or occasionally to Auschwitz, regardless of any paper or permit they held. The Nazis made a distinction between who would and would not be deported. People working in workshops were on the special category list of "essential workers." I do not know if or how they were compensated. They were really slave labourers. People paid millions to get work in a workshop, since having a workshop permit really meant having a permit to live. Some workshops made German uniforms and brooms. I believe that they subcontracted work from German industries. The broom factory became a major Resistance centre during the Warsaw uprising. There were also bakeries.

23 The Battle of Stalingrad was from November 1942 to January 1943.

*placowka*,[24] a group of Jews who, furnished with special passes, went to work on the Aryan side every day.

He reported to a *Wehrmacht Hauptmann*,[25] who was responsible for a *Wehrmacht* outpost that was barracked in what used to be a public school before the war. All public schools in Warsaw were built according to the same floor plan, *Umschlagplatz* being one of them. They were three-storey-high gray stone buildings with spacious rooms and big windows. Each had a basement. All of them were requisitioned as barracks for German soldiers.

A period of relative calm followed in the ghetto and for my family. My father went to work each day and brought us all the goodies unobtainable in the ghetto, such as bread, butter, ham, milk, and potatoes. My mother stayed at home, trying to keep up appearances. She repaired our shoes with leather cut out of the transmission belts that my father had salvaged from the machines in the factory. She polished our shoes with homemade polish that my father made from ashes and grease. She laundered and sewed our clothes.

Estusia trained and worked as a nurse in the Jewish hospital on Stawki Street, next to the *Umschlagplatz*. She used to go out, prim and elegant in her freshly starched and ironed white uniform and cap with a red cross on it. Every night, she used to come back, weary, dirty, and full of terrible stories of people dying due to lack of medication. She would wash her uniform and starch it with a homemade starch made out of raw potato peels.

I was still attending classes given by a group of teachers and students that had survived the massive deportation in July 1942.[26] We were promised report cards at the end of the war.

The Hashomer Hatzair organization was meanwhile working full speed both as a youth movement and to provide an orphanage, soup kitchen, and shelter for children whose parents had been deported. The soup kitchen was also a cover for the organization's political activities, but it was a bona fide soup kitchen nonetheless. As I was still attending school, I used to drop off the sandwich that my mother packed for my lunch as a donation for the orphaned children whose parents had been deported.

My role was to teach the children Polish. Many of them knew only Yiddish. We desperately needed money to maintain the shelter and the soup kitchen, which was housed at the headquarters of the Hashomer

---

24  Outpost.

25  German Army Captain.

26  This was the same deportation during which Estusia and I had hidden behind the door in 41 Mila Street.

Hatzair on Nalewki Street. The shelter's playground was the ruins of the bombed-out buildings on the corner of Muranowska and Nalewki.

We were told at our meetings how desperately Hashomer Hatzair needed money. So I went job hunting. I landed a job walking a baby in its stroller for an hour every day. I split my first pay, giving half to the organization and using the other half to buy a treat for my family: mouth-watering cakes filled with fresh whipped cream.[27] I remember how guilty I felt when my father complimented me on being so young yet contributing to the family's welfare. Little did he know that the idea was sparked by Hashomer Hatzair and the welfare I was concerned about was that of the orphans.

One day, my father did not return home. Estusia ran all over and found out that passes or no, my father's *placowka* had been taken directly to the *Umschlagplatz*. Estusia called and succeeded in reaching the *Wehrmacht Hauptmann* in charge of my father. She told him what had happened, begging him to help.

The saintly man (How I wish I could remember his name!) immediately went by car to the *Umschlagplatz*. He demanded that the young SS guard in front of the *Umschlagplatz* immediately deliver my father. The SS man refused, saying he needed a written order from SS headquarters. Pulling rank didn't help. The *Hauptmann* furiously told him that he would obtain orders and bring them first thing the next morning. Estusia and I told him that the trains were going daily and that tomorrow might be too late, but there was nothing more that the *Hauptmann* could do.

Inexplicably, my father succeeded in getting out of the *Umschlagplatz*. The next day, he reported to work as usual and begged the *Hauptmann* to take us out of the ghetto. My father suggested that my mother could do cleaning, housekeeping, and dusting for the soldiers, while Estusia and I could help him work on the crosses. The *Hauptmann* agreed and, having made a few calls, told my father to arrange the formalities with the Jewish *Arbeitsdienst*[28] in the ghetto.

The next day, my father and I presented ourselves at the *Arbeitsdienst*. When the officials there realized what was being arranged, they seized on

---

27 At the time, my father was working outside the Warsaw ghetto and could bring in milk for the family. If during this period, my father could bring milk in for his family, it's no surprise that, for the right price, anything was available from smugglers. Some Jewish bakers in the ghetto imported the raw materials and indeed made pastries, which were sold at astronomical prices in the ghetto.

28 Labour service.

the golden opportunity and persuaded the *Hauptmann* to arrange space for thirty people. The *Arbeitsdienst* didn't have "room" for Estusia, who had to remain in the ghetto, working in the hospital.[29]

It thus happened that thirty Jews were housed in the basement of the *Wehrmacht* barracks, working and living as Jews on the Aryan side, the men doing physical labour in the cemetery, the women working in the barracks, cooking, cleaning, and doing laundry. I helped my father paint in the incised letters on the crosses with black paint. In time, my father perfected his technique, substituting wood burning for carving and painting. While rain would wash out the black paint, woodburned letters better withstood the elements.

I was furnished with a special pass that enabled me to go to the ghetto once a week to visit Estusia. Meanwhile, Father would go to the head of the *Arbeitsdienst*, trying to persuade him to issue a pass for Estusia. Father even offered him money. Nothing doing. I used to go back and forth into the ghetto with other people. These people consisted mostly of families with children, but also of unattached young men who were smugglers. Estusia would wait for me at the entrance to the ghetto.

One day, as I entered the ghetto, one of these young smugglers saw Estusia waiting for me. He was smitten with her and told her that the next time he came back to the ghetto, he would have a pass for her to come out with the rest of us. I don't know how he got the pass, but he kept his promise, and Estusia was then able to come back with us to the barracks.

My special pass also allowed me to keep in touch with my comrades in Hashomer Hatzair. Security was strict within the organization, and I was tolerated only because on each visit I supplied them with food that I brought in from the outside. I noticed, on every visit, that the group had grown smaller. Some had perished in sniper skirmishes, some by disease, some by hunger. Very few died from deportations, since they had standing orders not to be taken alive.

The fighting conditions were terrible. In addition to the burden of responsibility and the danger of being in an underground movement, we were all alone, with no outside help. Our modest savings were laughable and fell far short of expenses.

With our limited resources, we concentrated our efforts where we could have the greatest practical impact. This turned out to be in

---

29 The *Arbeitsdienst* jumped at the opportunity to save themselves and their families. Since the number of people allowed to move to the Aryan side was limited, they excluded Estusia, including one of their own instead.

creating anti-deportation sentiment but did not translate into convincing people to fight.

However, as people began realizing that total deportation might be a possibility, construction of *Bunkiers* began on a grand scale in the ghetto. In what seemed an impossibly short time, *Bunkiers* were constructed, equipped with amenities to last a long period of time – *Bunkiers* with supplies of fresh water and fresh air, *Bunkiers* with their own, independent sources of electricity. Many were linked to other *Bunkiers*, creating a subterranean city.

Although an architectural feat, this was no solution to our situation. Our plight was not improved, merely prolonged. It was obvious that sooner or later the Germans would discover the *Bunkiers*. We knew that our feeble defences didn't matter much in terms of preventing a total deportation. But at least we knew that if we went, some of *them* would go too.

Lacking funds, we were forced to go from apartment to apartment armed with revolvers, extorting money for the resistance. But this, too, very quickly became futile. Falsely claiming that they were with the resistance organization, all kinds of bandits resorted to the same method for their own selfish sakes. Thus we abandoned our fundraising efforts.

The heavy, long, bloody days started. Our armaments were limited to hundreds of revolvers and a few machine guns, obtained with the help of the PPR (Polish Workers' Party, i.e., the Polish communist party) and the PPS (Polish Socialist Party). Days of cold waiting and feverish work, days and nights of dangerous forays, days of terrible *Blockades*, fires, and shooting, during which German heavy armour incessantly pounded the small cluster of houses. At night, the sky glowed red, the reflection of the burning houses in the ghetto.

But they were not able to burn and murder everywhere with impunity. There were incidents where heavy fighting took place, after which several of their bodies were left in the courtyards. Episodes like these happened often, but it was not enough.

If the whole ghetto had united in the revolt, we could have said that we had done our duty. But the uprising was of the young alone, who, with few exceptions, died in battle.

Arms and ammunition were dwindling quickly, and there was no question of obtaining new supplies. We had to hide. Unfortunately, there were not many of us left. We hid in *Bunkiers* for two days. Above ground, there was no sign of human life. Underground were the last of the Mohicans. Their turn came as well. Collaborators assisted the Germans until the last moments, throwing gas bombs into the *Bunkiers*. People fell, there were new victims. At best, half-choked, they climbed out of their *Bunkiers* to be taken by the Germans to the *Umschlagplatz*.

During one of these skirmishes, Estusia, I, and a boy from Hashomer Hatzair were hiding on the third floor of a three-storey building on Mila Street. It was a makeshift *Bunkier*, abandoned by its previous occupants. There was a big cupboard with a false back in the room. We went through the false back and hid in the next room.

When a house two doors down from us was set on fire,[30] the heat and smoke became so intense in our hiding place that we had to get out. We followed the boy, who seemed to know his way. We got to the window on the staircase, facing the courtyard where the Germans and Ukrainians were shooting their rifles at those jumping out of the windows. The smoke and heat were so bad that they couldn't shoot very accurately. Some people escaped. All the courtyards were joined, and if you knew your way you could disappear through the maze of the narrow passages linking them.

We were standing at the window when the boy yelled at us, *Jump!*

I stood there, paralyzed. My eyes were burning from the smoke, I could barely see. The three-storey drop terrified me, my clothes felt like they were burning on me. The soldiers shooting down there seemed to be looking and aiming right at me. All around, people were jumping, some to their deaths, their bodies littering the courtyard.

The boy screamed, *Jump!*

He jumped. Estusia jumped next. I was the last.

Incredibly, there were no broken bones, just scraped elbows and knees. We kept on running: through the shooting soldiers, jumping over bodies; through a narrow opening into the next courtyard, out in the open; through the glowing, hot ruins of burned-out houses. No tall buildings were left to block our view. We followed the boy blindly through the ruins.

Out of the corner of my eye, I could see other people running and jumping like rats, visible for a moment and disappearing the next. We finally reached a sewer. We parted company with our guide and saviour, whose name I don't even remember, and, by crawling through the sewers, managed to rejoin our parents in the *Wehrmacht* barracks.

Those who were not in a *Bunkier*, who did not hear the scream *Gas! Gas!*, who did not see the eyes bulging with insane fear, the twisted shapes, those who did not taste the sweetish-nauseating taste of gas penetrating

---

30 The Germans set all the houses in the ghetto on fire methodically, one after another. After the uprising, there wasn't a single house left standing. The fires were set deliberately to burn and smoke people out. People escaped, like us, by jumping from the windows and running away either into the sewers or the burning ruins or if they knew the secret passages to the Aryan side. Few people escaped. Most were shot on the spot or rounded up and deported.

one's pores and insides, those who did not feel that horrible pounding in the chest and head, those who did not crawl on all fours in the sewer's slime, unable to straighten out or squat down, but continuously crawling forward, feeling the gas, weakening and weakening, finally fainting at the manhole exit on the Aryan side: they could never understand how it felt.

Yes, the fact that we emerged alive from this exploding volcano could be called a miracle. We were the last to escape. After us, nobody came out, and there was nobody left. It was the beginning of May 1943.

My father made frantic efforts to place us with his non-Jewish friends and former employees. Isabella offered to take me. We knew that it was only a question of time before we would be rounded up and deported. Still, we were hoping against hope that maybe we wouldn't be.

It was too late. One morning, a detachment of SS-men surrounded the *Wehrmacht* barracks. They gave us time to pack our belongings. The *Wehrmacht* soldiers had tears in their eyes as they watched us being marched out. They pressed into our hands whatever they had, a bar of soap, a chocolate bar, a kerchief. Our *Hauptmann* was nowhere to be seen.

We were marched through the still-glowing ruins of the ghetto, the smoke and acrid smell of burned bodies in our eyes and noses. Nobody talked, nobody cried, we went like robots, only our feet moving, our hands shifting the heavy knapsacks on our backs that contained all our earthly possessions.

We were too numb to feel. We stopped at Stawki 6, at what used to be a public school in the good old days. It was a gray building, with spacious rooms and big windows, all designed to provide the optimum conditions for study and play for thousands of Polish students. Now every room was jam-packed.

We entered the *Umschlagplatz* and joined a sea of humanity. Everybody was sitting on the floor, hugging their possessions, families keeping together, waiting. It didn't seem to matter how long we waited. Everyone was too tired to care. Even the children were quiet. Then the trains came, and we were loaded onto them.

It is well known, and there is a lot of talk about, what happened in the Warsaw ghetto, what the prisoners in concentration camps went through, but little is known about the conditions of the "voyage" from Warsaw to the camps.

As a rule, fifty to sixty people were loaded into a boxcar. People could sit down, though with difficulty. On the second deportation from Warsaw, they loaded the boxcars with 150 to 170 people. Two days in closed cars without water or food! The lack of food didn't matter, because one couldn't eat under these conditions. But the lack of water! Our tongues felt like wooden wheels in our mouths. For a thousand Zloty, you could buy a glass of water at some stations, but it never reached anybody because the flailing arms grasping for it would spill and break it.

People were fainting and dying, one on top of another, relatives of the dying were hysterical; many went mad. There was no one to revive the fainted, there was nothing to revive them with, nor was there anyone left with enough presence of mind. Enough!

Coming out of the car, there were 120 left from our original 170. Half of them were mad, half-beaten-up, half-dead from thirst. No food or drink ever tasted as good to me as the mud under our feet when we jumped out of the railway car. It must have rained hard to have left this much water, which we scooped with our bare hands and which tasted like heavenly nectar. Drinking, or rather eating, this mud, little did I suspect that this place would become my first contact with the bitter reality and constant menace of life in the concentration camp.

# Majdanek[1]

## Arrival at Majdanek

It was raining on the May 1943 morning when we arrived at Majdanek. The door of the boxcar was pushed open, and suddenly we were blinded by the light of day. We had been in total darkness for how long, a day ... two ... three ... a lifetime.

There were screams outside: *Raus! Raus!*

Shots were being fired, dogs were barking. People were pushing toward the doors in panic, trampling each other in their haste. Estusia and I were standing, protecting our mother, who was sitting on the floor, totally exhausted. Both of us fell on top of her, pushed by the people running behind us, but we succeeded in saving her. We were the last ones to leave the car.

My mother admonished us to make sure that we took our knapsacks. All our possessions were in them. We jumped from the car to the ground – the distance seemed very great – then we helped our mother down. Once down, Estusia knelt on the ground and scooped up mud to quench her thirst. A riding crop descended on her back. They yelled at her, *Schnell! Schnell! Laufen! Laufen!*[2]

I held my mother's hand and we ran, people in front of us, people behind us. The road in front of us was strewn with abandoned valises, knapsacks, boxes, bundles, many burst open by trampling feet, the belongings muddy and dirty, clothes of all kinds, single shoes, food.

I couldn't run anymore with my knapsack, I dropped it, but my mother stubbornly kept hers on. Finally, we came to a stop and then proceeded slowly

---

1 This section of the chapter consists of memoirs written between 1991 and 1994 in Ottawa, Canada. Majdanek *Konzentrationslager* ("concentration camp") was in the vicinity of Lublin.

2 "Hurry! Hurry! Run! Run!"

to follow the people ahead of us. We didn't know and cared less about what was happening ahead of us, glad to have a chance to catch our breath.

On our right was a tall wire fence. Behind this fence were emaciated men, their heads shaven, wearing funny-looking uniforms with blue and gray vertical stripes. They were yelling to us. At first, I could not understand what they were saying.

Then I realized that they were screaming in Yiddish and Polish: *Throw us your money, your jewels, your valuables! You won't be needing them where you are going!*

*It must be an insane asylum,* I thought to myself. I ignored them.

We followed the crowd. Something was yelled in front of us – the men were to be separated from the women and children. Women to the left, men to the right. We advanced slowly. We lost track of my father and Estusia. I was holding my mother's hand all the time. A young SS officer on my left beckoned to me. I pulled my mother with me. He gestured to me to leave my mother. I let go. He pointed with his finger for me to go to the right. I turned back to get my mother, but she was gone, lost in the crowd.

Alone, I followed the rest into a wooden barrack, empty of all furnishings but full of women. Screaming uniformed SS women told us to get undressed and leave all our clothes on the floor. We could keep our shoes.

I found Estusia. We were so relieved to find each other. She asked me about our mother; I said she was still outside. The SS women told us to give them all our money and valuables. I had on a plaid dress with a green leather belt. My mother had sewn gold coins and American dollars into the belt. I was tempted to put the belt inside my shoes, which I was carrying in my hand. But the screams and the whipping ahead of me so scared me that I threw my belt away.

We proceeded to the showers, a mass of naked females. From there, we went to a room where we were given underwear and dresses. Once dressed, we were directed to a wooden barrack. At the door, each of us was given a thin gray blanket, a tin spoon, and a bowl. As we passed inside, we had to hold out our bowls, which were filled with a thin, warm soup. It tasted like nectar to our parched throats. Then we sat on the floor, as there was no furniture of any kind in this dark barrack. The light from outside came through narrow slits under the roof.

We spent the night on the floor, sleeping soundly. We were woken abruptly in the middle of the night, at about 4 a.m. and driven outside to stand at *Appel.*[3]

---

3  Roll call.

It was freezing outside. Even though it was spring, the wind was howling and cut right through us. Estusia and I clung to each other for warmth. We stood there for hours. For the first time in my life, I saw the sun rise. We were standing on a hill. There was nothing on the horizon but barren plain, as far as the eye could see.

I was amazed to see that the clouds moving across the sun created shadows on the earth that knit a quilt of light and dark patches, beautiful and ever changing. Finally, the *Appel* over, we were given a warm, nondescript drink that went under the name of "tea" and a piece of bread.

Estusia and I decided that we would volunteer for work outside the camp to look for the other camps that the Czech prisoners had told us about. Maybe we would find our parents.

## In Majdanek[4]

We inquired persistently about the fate of our parents. Both my sister and I were cured of our pestering by the old-timers in the camp, orderly and kindly Czech political prisoners, who put us off by telling us that our parents were not far away, in other camps reserved for the elderly. The work was lighter for them there. We desperately wanted to believe them. Every morning we volunteered for *Aussenkommandos*[5] in the hope of getting a glimpse of the other camps and meeting people from them.

We were awakened in pitch darkness by the yells and shouting of the German female wardens. They were equipped with riding crops and wore shining, soft, knee-high leather boots; they used both crops and boots freely to drive us out of our barracks for *Appel.*

We learned quickly not to linger behind, and not to hurry too much either. If you lingered too long, you felt the riding crop or the boot or both. If you hurried too much, you would be in the first row of five women. No one wanted to be in the first row. Being in the first row meant being exposed to the howling winds, unprotected by the girl in front of you, exposed to the searching looks of guards and wardens, to be selected, who knows for what?

---

4 This section of the chapter consists of memoirs first published in *The Ottawa Jewish Bulletin* in March 1975 under the title, "Holocaust Diary by Hagar" (my name in the Hashomer Hatzair). It has been edited for inclusion here.

5 Slave labour details that worked outside the camp.

We used to stand on *Appel* for hours and hours. By the end of the *Appel*, it didn't matter any more for which *Kommando*[6] you were picked. Anything was better than standing, and the opportunity to move our numb toes and fingers was sweet indeed.

I was assured by more experienced girls that my first assignment in Majdanek was a lucky one indeed. It was called the "latrine *Kommando.*" That is exactly what it was. We were supposed to empty the makeshift camp latrines into wagons, then push the wagons outside the camp to fertilize the neighbouring fields.

The latrines were simply holes dug in the ground, set behind a wooden wall on the camp side but facing the electrified fence that delineated the camp's boundary. This meant that the latrines were exposed to the full view of the German sentries, who leered at us and made lewd comments from the watchtowers. After a while, I got used to and accepted them as part of the general surroundings. They didn't matter.

What mattered were the contents of the latrine wagon. The wagons were shaped like small oblong trunks on four wheels. There were two long handles in front, to which I suppose one could harness a horse.

Instead of horses, two girls pulled the wagon from the front, two pushed from the sides and two pushed from behind. Using shovels and buckets, we loaded the wagon through a hole on the top. We would load them half-full (if nobody was too close to watch) and run them into the fields. Half-full, the wagons were not too heavy.

We were anxious to get out of the camp. It just *smelled* different on the other side. We emptied the contents of the wagon through a hose at the back. Then one of us had to climb on top and, sticking a shovel through the top hole, push the muck left at the bottom on through toward the hose. Before I knew what was happening, I was the chosen one.

*Sucker!* I muttered and swore under my breath – *He who hesitates!*

I was sitting on top, straddling the wagon, pushing the muck with my shovel, looking to see how much was left, when, lo and behold, I saw something shiny. A gold coin!

*Mine! All mine!* I thought.

I didn't hesitate to put my hand in to grab it. I held it tight in the palm of my hand. I couldn't keep my excitement to myself: I started shouting and calling to my sister. She came running, startled, afraid

---

6  Slave labour detail.

something had happened to me. I got off the wagon, opened my palm, and showed her.

*Look! Look what I got!*

We were standing, huddled together, speechless.

Suddenly a cool voice said calmly, *Half of it is mine.*

We both looked up into the set face. It was the girl next to us.

Finally, I burst out, *What do you mean, half of it is yours?*

*It says so in the book*, she said. *If I witness a find, half of it belongs to me. Anyway, if you don't share, I shall report you.*

Well, that was it. We walked toward the pump to hose out the wagon. The pump was also used by farmers. As it happened, we saw a farmer. The girl, who was sticking to us like glue, called out to him. He obviously was familiar with the routine. Trembling, I showed him the coin. He scratched his head.

Then he said, *O.K. I will give you a half loaf of bread.*

The girl was bold. *Nothing doing. You will give us a half loaf of bread and a big piece of meat.*

He didn't argue. It was as dangerous for him to be found near us as it was for us near him. He gave us our meat and bread and hurried away. We pushed the bread and meat under our dresses. I couldn't help laughing. I just looked nicely padded, no more and no less.

The way back was agonizing. The other girls were in no hurry to get back to camp. They often stopped to pull out the horseradish roots that abounded in the fields. Remembering the hot taste of grated horseradish, I couldn't understand how they could eat it.

My curiosity got the better of me. I stopped to pick one, wiped it on the sleeve of my dress, and bit into it. My, did it taste good! It wasn't hot at all, but tender and crunchy.

We went on looking down in search of the roots and around in search of other camps. The roots were there, but the camps were not. Well, it was a good day. Maybe we would find the camp of the old people tomorrow. We looked for four months in Majdanek. We looked, never admitting to each other that there were no camps for older people.

In August, a transport of Greek Jewish girls came to Majdanek from Auschwitz. They told us that they had been transferred to Majdanek because they were suffering from malaria and couldn't stand the Auschwitz climate. Our hopes rose. The horror stories we had heard were not true after all. Surely we would meet our parents in Auschwitz. We knew that we were going in the next transport because one had already left.

We couldn't wait to get to Auschwitz. The day came one bright September morning.[7] But we didn't find our parents. They weren't there. Where were they?

---

7  Unlike the circumstances of the transfer of my cousin, Sonia, and Sonia's sister, where the two women volunteered to go to Auschwitz, my sister and I were simply told that we would be transferred. My transfer immediately succeeded a transfer of Greek women from Auschwitz to Majdanek. These women were supposedly transferred for "health reasons" – they had contracted malaria, and the "climate was better at Majdanek." Of course, this was a lie, but it succeeded in removing any apprehension that we felt about going to Auschwitz. Further, unlike the transport from Warsaw to Majdanek, conditions in the cattle cars in which we were moved from Majdanek to Auschwitz were much better. The doors were open. I remember hanging my legs out the door. There was straw on the floors. We were given rations. We were neither hungry nor thirsty during the trip.

# Auschwitz[1]

Wires, a ditch filled with dirty slime, and another row of wires. On the wires was a little plaque: *Achtung! Lebens Gefahr!*[2] Aha! That means the wires are electrified. So this is Auschwitz.

Behind the wires, in neat lines, are row upon row of red brick buildings with tiny windows. But these windows do not allow fresh air to come in, since they are permanently closed. This is on one side of the camp. On the other side are wooden barracks painted green. These have no windows at all. In front of each *Block*[3] is a stretch of sand circled with bricks. In the middle, a tree that resembles a mop. This constitutes what is proudly called a "garden." Ah, the garden! Here is where I first got it!

I was very tired when we arrived, so I sat on top of one of the bricks. I had hardly sat down when a girl came running toward me and slapped me in the face. At first, I didn't know what was happening, then I thought, *It must be a crazy woman! Why is she hitting me?*

But when she slapped me again, I got up furious, yelling, *How dare you hit me, in the face yet?*

In answer, she slapped me for the third time, so hard that I toppled over. I heard laughter around me. When I got up and wiped my bleeding lip, I heard, as through a mist, that one is not allowed to sit on top of the garden. I looked around to find the garden but could see nothing. It was only later that I learned that I was indeed sitting on "it." I noticed that in the camp first you get a beating and then, if you are lucky, an explanation. More often no explanation is forthcoming. You got it, keep it, and don't talk or you will get more.

---

1 This chapter consists of diary material written in the Ardennes, Belgium, in July 1945.

2 "Attention ! Life Threatening!"

3 Barrack.

We are standing in front of a "sauna." What is a sauna? The sauna is a bath. Here you got clean underwear, clean clothes, and a shower.

There are many of us. They let us in by the hundreds. I am so tired that I can hardly stand on my feet. I can't wait for the hot shower. Finally it is our turn. A long, wide corridor stretches in front of us, all covered with discarded clothing. Deafening screams greet us.

*Quick! Quick! Take off all your clothes! Not here, there! Where are you climbing, you Polish swine?!*

Screams, beatings. I get undressed as quickly as I can to escape these screams which have rendered me half-conscious. I run blindly, naked toward the noise of running water and showers.

*Hop to it! Stop! Not so fast! Back! Haircut!*

*Why? My hair is clean!*

Laughter answers me. I look around and I see young girls with scissors and clippers cutting hair off clean to the scalp. I sit on a stool, and I try to tell myself that it is nothing. But when the cold scissors touch my scalp and my hair slowly falls down, I can't help it, and my tears fall down, mixed with my black curls. Curls fall down and tears fall down. Curls so warm, tears so warm, and the scissors so cold. Brrr! Finished. I run my hand over my head. Nothing.

*Estusia,* I call my sister, *where are you?*

*Here!*

*Where?*

*But here.*

She stands in front of me, but I do not recognize her. She looks like a boy. Two large green eyes, pale face, and totally bald, because there is no more hair.

Further along are two more girls. One writes down our first names and family names and the other, with the help of a pen dipped in ink, is tattooing numbers on our left arms. Mine is 48150,[4] Estusia's 48149.

We go to the shower. We wait a few seconds. Water cold as ice falls on us. We jump away, only to be drenched with ice-cold water poured on us from buckets by the screaming witches all around us. Well, there is no choice. Teeth chattering, we begin to soap ourselves. All soaped up, we want to rinse. No more water. Do what you want.

---

4 The girl that tattooed my number told me that, because the digits of my number added to 18 (the sum of the numbers associated with the Hebrew letters of the word "Chai"), that I would live. "Chai" in Hebrew means "life."

To the swishing noise of riding crops on naked bodies we are chased forward. We crowd together to put something on as soon as possible; wet and cold, we tremble like jelly. And here they beat us again.

*Don't push!*

The whole naked group moves like a living wave. Where there is a riding crop, there is a hollow in the crowd. Everybody runs away as far as they can. And when the riding crop is turned the other way, everybody runs back. Finally, they throw something into our faces and push us forward.

*Why do they push? We are going on our own!*

*Plash! Smack!*

*You see, I told you not to talk.*

Fuming with anger, I look at what I was given. A slip, panties. But something is crawling over the slip and the panties.

*Estusia, what is it?* I show her the little vermin.

We both look carefully, closely. They have to be lice. Phew! We throw the rags away and go forward for dresses.

*Dresses? You must have forgotten you are in a prison-camp, not at home!*

We get male Russian uniforms, shirts and pants. Everything is too large; there is no way to tighten or button them. The coarse, hard material scratches our skin. We get colourful stockings: I get one white and one green. But we do get beautiful silk kerchiefs[5] for our heads. On our feet, we wear wooden clogs that feel like clay poles and make a deafening noise with each step we take.

At last, the washing ritual over, we were marched into our *Block*. It became clear that the screaming monkeys were actually old-timers, who had been in the camp since its beginning, which meant almost a year. They had suffered a great deal, but had by now secured administrative jobs in the camp. They took out their rage on us, the newcomers. As if it were our fault that they were caught before us. They were the ones who led us into the *Block*.

The first impression upon entering the *Block*[6] was surprisingly pleasant: a large entrance; over it a little window covered with an attractive mesh

---

5  Estusia and I arrived immediately after a group of Russian prisoners had been murdered. We were given their uniforms. There were no hats. Instead, we got silk kerchiefs looted from Jews who had arrived on the transports and who had been subsequently murdered. The Jews who had come on the transports had brought the best of what they had.

6  To the left as you entered Auschwitz were brick barracks. I think that they once might have been stables. Their entrance area was very nice, but when you went further inside it was just awful. To the right as you entered the camp were wooden barracks, reserved

curtain; inside were rows of two- and three-storey-high wooden bunk beds covered with blankets whose colours matched the curtains. Arranged in the middle of the hall were several wooden stools, covered with kerchiefs in colourful designs. The walls were whitewashed: painted on them were the numbers of the *Stube*[7] and the sign, *"Ruhe im Block."*[8]

The *Stube* were laid out like the letter *H*. There were two parallel corridors consisting of stalls facing one another. One corridor was in the front of the *Block*, one in the rear, connected by a walk-through corridor. The walls of these corridors consisted of two-storey-high brick stalls, which were called *Koja*.[9] Each *Koja* was one and a half metres wide by two metres high. It served as a bed for six to eight persons. Each stall held two straw mattresses and two thin blankets. The dirt and stench were overwhelming.

Happy that finally we had a place to rest our tired bones, we fell like corpses on the bed. There were eight of us. My sister and I lay close together, clutching at each other, trying to take as little space as possible. We lay like this for a few minutes in a heavy, half-dreaming stupor.

Suddenly, I feel an enormous weight on me. I lift my head, and I see that somebody is sleeping on top of me. Politely, I ask her to move. I can't support her. She doesn't hear. I shake her a little.

Suddenly, she kicks my legs up like a football and screams, *Oh! Oh! She is killing me! She is kicking me! Oh! Oh! I am dying, Madam Blockhova!*[10]

I look at her. I don't understand. She falls on top of *me* with all her weight, squeezes the breath out of me, and she yells that I am killing *her*.

*Estusia,* I call to her quietly, *I can't stand it any more.*

With Estusia's help, I somehow sit down, my back against the brick wall, my knees under my chin. The crazy one is still screaming and

---

for non-Jews: Poles, Germans, and "VIPs." The wooden barracks were much less unpleasant and were equipped with bunk beds. There were non-Jews on the brick barrack side too, but mostly they accommodated those in special *Kommandos*, people who worked in the "sauna." When we first arrived, we were in *Lager A* (Camp *A*), quartered in these brick barracks. When we later volunteered to work in the Union munitions factory in *Lager B*, we stayed for a short time in one of the wooden barracks, where we slept two to a bunk. The *Blockhova* was a non-Jew. Estusia caught typhus during this period in the wooden barracks. Then we were moved into the brick barracks for the Union slave labourers.

7 Section of barracks.

8 "Quiet in the Block!"

9 Pronounced *Ko-ya.*

10 In German, *Blockhova* is *Blockälteste*, the senior woman prisoner in charge of a block of barracks.

"Koja" (bed) in Auschwitz K.Z.
Eight prisoners slept on top, eight in the middle and eight at the bottom.

groaning. I feel my cheeks redden in embarrassment. People may believe that I really hit her. But now I hear cries and screams from all the other *Koja*. Here and there, the mattresses are flying. The women's yelling is answered by a *Shtubhova*.[11] Every *Stube* has its *Shtubhova*.

*What is going on here!?*

*Madam Shtubhova! She took my blanket!*

*It's a lie! It's my blanket!*

As the *Shtubhova* yells, the women continue their screaming, each trying to pull the blanket over to her side. A rag really, the blanket tears in two. The *Shtubhova* calls the *Blockhova*, who comes but does not ask any questions. Using her belt, she strikes right and left. She tells the two fighting women to kneel in the middle of the *Block* with their hands up. There is quiet for five minutes. Then the screams start all over again. Suddenly, the air is penetrated by a shrill whistle.

*Zahlappel! Alle raus!*[12]

We are thrown outside. We blink our eyes from the sudden light and look around. Through the main gate come columns and columns of women in rows of five. Those are the *Kommandos* returning from work.

You can feel their weariness in their heavy step and dusty clothes. All so thin, so strange, they don't look like women at all. They walk and sing.[13] They shuffle their naked feet over sharp pebbles and sand, holding their shoes in their hands. Their hands are red, swollen, burned. They walk, lugging big baskets loaded to the top with some kind of nettle-like plant. All day long, in the heat, under the riding crops of German uniformed guards and *Kapos*,[14] the prisoners have to collect the stuff with their bare hands. It is used as greens in our soup. They go by. They disappear. Although you can hear them singing, they look like ghosts.

Here comes another *Kommando*. But this one is quite different. They walk smartly from afar in orderly rows, their white, pink, and blue kerchiefs glistening in the sun. They sing loudly. They are dressed beautifully: clean, freshly pressed blouses; pleated skirts; silk stockings and leather shoes. This is the *Kanada Kommando*,[15] the "elite" of the camp. They work at sorting the belongings stolen from those arriving in on the transports. At

---

11  Female inmate in charge of a section of barrack *(Stube)*.

12  "Roll call, everyone outside!"

13  All *Kommandos* were ordered to sing.

14  Prisoner-trusty, a prisoner given special privileges for good behaviour.

15  It was called "Kanada" after Canada, a land supposed to be of untold wealth.

the same time, they "organize," meaning they loot. This is how they have beautiful clothes to wear and how they can get anything they want to eat in exchange for the things they succeed in smuggling into camp.

Yet in spite of the fact that they have it so well and that they look so different from the *Aussenkommandos*, those who work outside the camp, there is one thing that links them together – and not only these two *Kommandos*, but everybody in the camp. When you look in their eyes, they appear to be blind. But they are not blind. Their dead eyes reflect their dead souls.

One after another, the *Kommandos* parade before us, regiments of women conscripted for hard physical labour. Deprived of free will, of free thought, under the influence of the bromides mixed into their food, they become compliant tools in the hands of criminals and obligingly execute all their orders without any resistance. Existing on rations too little to live on and too much to die from, the unfortunates wander between life and death. They exist as if they are balanced upon a huge scale in the sky, subjected to the merciful or cruel whims of those who have power over them. The mere crook of a finger tips the scale one way or another.

I stand at *Appel*. We all do. The *Appel* drags on indefinitely. Our legs fall asleep under us and we get lightheaded. When will it end? These *Appel*s sapped our remaining energy.

Finally, so long awaited, *Abtreten!*[16]

Now we line up in front of the *Block* doors and, coming in, receive our dinner. Officially, we were supposed to get a quarter of a loaf of bread and something else. But our *Block* staff took care to steal our rations so that we received only a fifth or a sixth of a loaf. Everybody pushes and crowds. After a long *Appel,* everybody wants to be inside as soon as possible.

I hold my portion with both hands to make sure that nobody grabs it from me, and run to our *Koja*. I stand there, stupefied. There is a veritable revolution inside the *Block*. Mattresses and blankets are flying. The air is full of dust. Our *Koja* is bare wooden planks. No mattress. No blankets. What to do? I do what the others do. I pull a blanket and a mattress from the nearest empty *Koja* and sit on it so that nobody can take it away from me.

Slowly the *Block* fills up. I hear cries and sobs everywhere. Some *Kojas* have ten blankets, some have none, somebody had their "dinner" stolen from them. After the day-long fast, we feel our throats cramp convulsively. We eat our bread quickly. All of it. All of it. We don't leave anything for tomorrow. We reassure ourselves that this way nobody can steal it from

---

16 "Retire!" (back to the *Block*).

us during the night. The best way is to hold it in our stomachs. In spite of this reassurance, something in our hearts wonders, *What will happen tomorrow morning?* Never mind, tomorrow we may be dead. But hunger tortures us, and the spectre of tomorrow doesn't want to disappear.

Slowly it becomes dark. Exhausted from the day's events, people fall asleep. But I can't sleep. I am lying down, my eyes wide open, listening to the night noises. The aroma of wonderful cooking drifts from the *Brotkammer.*[17] It irritates my nostrils, and my mouth waters.

*Those are our stolen portions of margarine,* I think to myself.

In the *Koja* opposite, somebody stands up on the top bed. She takes a soup bowl, urinates into it, and without troubling to climb down, pours the contents onto the floor. I feel nauseated, close to vomiting. I envy my sleeping comrades, who snore to different tunes. I try to fall asleep but can't. It is an awful feeling, not to be able to fall asleep, to see, hear, and smell everything around you.

Armies of lice are crawling all over me, biting me, drawing blood. I am so squashed that I can't free my hand to scratch myself. I twist and turn and eventually am able to free one hand to scratch. Oh, what a relief! Slowly, my eyes close. I see a whole golden loaf of bread. A whole loaf of bread for me alone! I grab it with both my hands to sink my teeth into it, when the shrill of the whistle wakes me up. I close my eyes to see my treasure once more, but my dream has flitted away, leaving me miserably awake. *Oh, why didn't I have time just for one bite?*

Again there are long hours of standing at *Appel.* They chase us out at 4 a.m., in the middle of the night. We stand, huddling together, clapping our hands and stomping our feet to keep warm. We have to wait a long, long time until daybreak, until the SS *Aufseherin*[18] comes to count us. Then we have to stand at attention, spaced far from each other in neat rows of five.

*Yes, she is nice and warm,* I think to myself with hate, looking at her tall shining boots, her warm well-fitting green uniform and black cape. She counts once. It doesn't add up. She counts again. We grow stiff and cold. Somebody faints. Those standing nearby hold her up and ask the *Shtubhova* for a glass of water.

*Let her die!* comes the answer.

---

17 The room where food was stored and distributed.

18 Uniformed female work supervisor and guard.

Finally, *Abtreten*. We want to move, to go, but our stiff legs refuse our brains' command. We can't move them. A few minutes pass before we can make the first step.

*Everybody to the Wiese!* screams the *Blockhova*.

*Wiese* (meadow) means a piece of ground behind the barrack enclosed by a wire. The newcomers to the camp go through a period of quarantine and don't work. The quarantine means that, come rain or shine, we have to sit in this *Wiese* all day long. It resembles an island of people stricken with leprosy.

The whole place is filled with living corpses. Some are sitting, exploring themselves for lice, exposing flesh covered with pimples and boils. Others are stretched out unmoving on the ground, thin as string, insects and flies hovering over them, lips scorched with fever, their eyes invisible beneath swollen faces. Their hands and feet are also swollen, covered with wounds and sores.

The clatter here is a mixture of all the European languages. It is a veritable Tower of Babel. Quarrelsome, wasted by dysentery, malaria, and scabies, the Greek girls, knowing only the Greek language, are trying to make themselves understood by movement and gesture. But nobody understands them, nor cares to try. Their beautiful big black eyes misted by fever and pain, their lively southern temperaments take on a quarrelsome and nasty bent. They don't let anybody talk to them. They sob. They cry. They scratch at each other.

There is no shortage of French girls, their faces still bearing the colour of lipstick and cosmetics. There are girls from Belgium and Holland as well. Due to the language difficulties, all the nationalities keep to themselves, in separate groups.

On one side is a group of the much-disliked German Jewish girls. Being German, they feel that they deserve special respect and esteem. Should one of them obtain any position of power in the camp, she behaves worse toward other prisoners than do the uniformed German guards. Not to mention the camp's Slovakian and Polish old-timers, who had a great deal of power and controlled the life in the camp according to their own indisputable whims.

My sister and I sit down as far away from everybody as possible. We are silent. There is nothing to talk about. In spite of myself, my gaze is drawn to the shapes around me. Not far away from me, a young girl shakes convulsively with spasms of malaria. She lies down with her head in the sand, her eyes closed, her body bouncing off the ground like a ball.

Farther on sits another girl, her head tucked under her armpit, her hand trembling as she throws live lice to the ground. Under her turned-up slip you could see her naked body, all eaten up by lice and scabies. I turn my head away and start to scratch. I don't know if it was just the suggestion or if something really bit me.

On the other side of me sit two women, who knows, maybe a mother and a daughter or maybe two sisters just like us, or maybe simply two unfortunate beings thrown together by a tragic fate. You could see that one of them was consumed by fever, maybe dysentery, maybe typhoid. The other, tears in her eyes, looks upon her companion's suffering and tries to help her by putting a canteen with muddy water to her lips. She doesn't realize that she is feeding her poison.

I felt so awful. *Who knows,* I thought, *what we would look like in a few days?* I looked at my sister. She was so changed just by her clipped hair. Our gazes met and quickly we turned our heads away. We were petrified. Petrified about what awaited us.[19]

*Don't worry,* I said, *Don't worry. You will see. It will be all right. It has to be.*

She smiled weakly.

Hunger twisted our guts. At noon, a whistle penetrated the air, announcing lunch. Lunch consisted of half a litre of oily warm water. But how good it tasted! And again *Wiese* until *Appel*. Days went by in pain, hunger, and fear amid the torment of the lengthy standing at *Appel*, the meagre supper, the fighting for blankets.

One day, they were out grabbing people for work. They took Estusia and me. We had to load a cart with garbage and push it out of the camp. There were eight of us, weak and exhausted, and the cart was heavy when fully loaded. We all pushed hard, but the cart wouldn't move.

The *Kapo*'s blows descend like hail on our backs. And every blow is ever so more painful since our backs were just skin and bones. Finally, the cart budged. We push hard and it moves toward the gates, to the *Blockführerstube,*[20] which was also where the *Kapo* would go to report. At the *Blockführerstube*, we are assigned a uniformed male guard with a dog.

We continue walking and pushing. The wheels of the cart creak. The sand crackles under our feet. Covered with sweat, we continue to push the cart, unable to straighten our aching backs. Our *Kapo* and the guard are having a wonderful time. Now they find a new entertainment: they sick the dog on us. Propelled by fear, we quicken our step, too terrified to look back at the dog's bloodshot eyes and its glistening fangs.

---

19 This "quarantine" period, during which prisoners were not assigned jobs, served as a kind of boot camp and so served as a "passive selection."

20 Guardhouse at the camp gates.

Worked into a frenzy, the dog jumps on one of the girls and buries its teeth in her. There is a terrible scream; the girl falls down. The two sadists laugh aloud. My eyes brim with tears and my fists clench. But there was no choice. I hang my head and go on. The wheels creak, the two laugh uproariously, and the dog runs beside them, wagging its tail. A corpse is left behind on the road. We return with a lighter cart but a heavier heart. Well, what matters a corpse? One more or less makes no difference.

That evening, the *Block* secretary announced the registration of all the Greek girls. Well, it did not concern me. I lay down and scratched. What a pleasure! I scratched nervously, passionately, until I drew blood.

One day, while we were on *Appel,* the *Lagerälteste*[21] whistle announced *Blocksperre,* which meant that everybody had to stay inside the *Block.* Nobody was allowed out.[22]

We go into the *Block,* on the one hand happy that we don't have to go out to work, on the other, torn by anxiety. What was going to happen? It is quieter than usual in the *Block.* Everybody is lying down in exhausted tension. The *Block* secretary yells: *All Greek girls out!* What for, I ask myself. A stir begins in the *Kojas.* The Greek girls come down. Not all of them: some continue to lie down and sob loudly; others hide deeply under mattresses and blankets. But the *Shtubhovas* know their charges. They find them, pull them out with screams and beatings. The vile creatures are sending these young and healthy beings, who have the same right to live as they do, to their deaths.

Isn't it enough that the barbarians are doing it, do these prisoners have to help? But they are no longer human; they don't care that they pay for their own lives with the death of thousands of others. Their own survival comes at any price. I turn my head and squeeze my forehead, nose, and lips to the cool pane of the little window.

*Egoism is the engine of human life* – Friedrich Engels' words pound in my head.[23] *Egoism is the engine of human life* – the bloody syllables dance in front of my eyes, taking on the shapes of these unbridled sadists with riding crops in their hands, the shape of all the bureaucrats that the barbarians changed into their willing tools, the shapes of the ghosts of all their murdered, exhausted victims. I see little groups walking as if at funerals. But strange funerals.

---

21 Camp overseer. The *Lagerälteste* was a prisoner who carried out the orders of the *Lagerkommandant* (the death camp's commandant).

22 *Blocksperre* would accompany selections. It was really a sort of lock-down.

23 This was a quote that I had learned during my involvement with the Hashomir Hatzair.

Funerals of the living. The *Shtubhovas* and *Blockhovas* form a guard around those groups and lead them toward *Block* 25.[24]

*Block* 25 was surrounded by a tall brick wall with heavy iron gates. Iron bars were set in its tiny windows. Despairing mothers, sisters, or other relatives gathered in front of *Block* 25, stretching their hands out to those inside. How often they crawled at the feet of the SS guards, begging to be taken to their death as well, to die together with those dear to them! But the answer was either a hard kick by an SS man's boot or the sharp end of a lash. Inside were hundreds condemned to death. But why? What for? Because they were young, because they broke under impossible conditions, because on their birth certificates was a small little word – "*Jew*."

Hands grabbed at the iron grates in vain, trying to break them. Too weak, too weak! They hit their heads against the walls, they trembled at each creak of the door, at the sound of heavy, booted steps. Here and there sat girls with silly grins on their faces, laughing incessantly. They were the lucky ones. They had lost their minds and didn't realize what was going on around them. Others were running from one corner to the other, froth on their mouths, their eyes insane with fear. Hysterical sobs were mixed with wild, satanic, mad laughter, all to the accompaniment of the thuds of heads hitting against the walls in dumb helplessness.

What is hell compared to your *Block* 25? Is there a worse torture than that of a human being who is quite consciously awaiting forthcoming death for no reason at all? And when the shape of an executioner with a riding crop or a gun in his hand appears in the dark rectangle of the door, everybody scurries into the corners. There is no one to oppose him. His shape seemed to hypnotize them. But it didn't: their own fear hypnotized them. They had been too long exposed to thoughts of death. They waited too long, every second in mortal fear that Death was approaching. When it came, they had no strength left to fight it.

Like sleep-walkers they mounted the waiting trucks willingly, and were driven to the innocent-looking little houses[25] outside the camp, disappearing inside them. Then red tongues of fire and black smoke gushed from the tall chimneys of the little houses – their souls escaping into the infinite expanse.

-------------------

24  *Block* 25 served as a collection point for victims of selections before they were murdered.

25  These were the crematoria. Though large complexes, since they were partially underground, from the perspective of someone in the camp they looked like little houses with tall chimneys.

The legion of those left over, lucky, specially chosen, continued to struggle in this hell, as they constructed their own graves and cemeteries. They waited for the day when the trucks would come for them, and then they, too, would follow their dead comrades. Often heads turned involuntarily toward these innocent little houses, surrounded by green shrubs, with the tall, tall chimneys sprouting into the sky, where the sky was always black and the acrid smell of burned bones penetrated the air and irritated the nostrils. *Yes,* we smiled cynically, *this is our future.*

Across from our camp on one side stretched the men's camp.

Standing at *Appel*, we could see rows of men in identical blue-gray striped coats going to and from work. They lived just like we did. They suffered the same, but separately from us. But the crematoria were shared by all. Looking at the men, I could see the same bent, tired figures, the same expressionless faces, hear the same characteristic clap of wooden clogs.

But one day we no longer saw the sad rows of blue-gray coats, nor did we hear the clap of the clogs to which we were by now so accustomed. I felt as if I had been robbed of something, as if a piece of me had been torn away. They were transferred to another camp. We would occupy the *Blocks* vacated by them. One camp was insufficient for us.

New transports were arriving continuously, from Belgium, France, Holland, and Poland. To take them to the gas chambers directly would be too easy a death for them. To graduate from the school of life, they first had to go through a school of torment. Only then would they be liberated, to finish it all there, in the little houses with big chimneys.

But only the young and strong came into camp. The children and elderly were annihilated, gassed immediately. Room was needed for the new arrivals. We were no longer newcomers. Hundreds and hundreds came after us.

Now it was our turn as old-timers, as experienced and seasoned prisoners, to greet the new arrivals. But not in the way we were greeted. We sympathized with them, we saw in them living greetings from the outside world. The world! Slowly we had begun to forget that a thing like the world ever existed.

We often spoke with them. They asked us about their families that had been taken away in the trucks. We smiled. What could we tell them? If we told them the truth, they wouldn't believe us. The move to the other camp started.[26] We were moved according to assignment in *Kommandos*. Estusia and I were not attached to any particular *Kommando*; we were tossed like balls from one *Kommando* to another, whether we were needed or not.

---

26  This was our move from *Lager A* to *Lager B*.

It was out of the question for us to stay in the *Block*. No, if we couldn't find other work, we were made to carry heavy bricks. We had to run with this heavy load to the rhythm of a swishing lash. Whoever fell would not get up again. And then we had to carry the bricks back. We decided at all costs to "normalize" our lives.

On a whim we volunteered to join a *Kommando* of "metallurgists." Rumour had it that they were going to construct a factory in *Lager B* to make buttons, combs, and so forth. Before moving to the other camp, we had, like the other *Kommandos*, to undergo a "medical exam," in other words, a selection.[27]

We go to the sauna. With pleasure we get rid of our filthy, stiff, lice-covered rags. We step into another large room. There are nothing but stairs. A cold draft penetrates through the broken windowpanes.

We sit on the stairs, naked, trembling, chilled to the bone, our teeth chattering. Seldom can one see a clean body, a body not marred by scratches or scabies. Only skin and bones. The heads, smooth-shaven heads, are beginning to be covered again with a thin layer of new-growth hair. Not at all resembling living human beings, we look like one living mass of corpses.

At the sound of a command, we go over, or rather we spill over, to the showers. The water comes down. Luckily, knowing from experience, we don't soap ourselves. Indeed, after a minute of cold shower, the water is turned off. Again, many hours of exhausting waiting. We get lightheaded from hunger, our bodies are indescribably tired, and we experience a feeling of total apathy. Oh, if only we had something hot to gulp, or a small piece of blanket! From a remote hall, we hear echoes of the conversation and laughter of flirting SS men and SS women. Suddenly, we hear anxious whispers.

*Tauber! Tauber is here!*

Cold shivers go right through me. On his walks through the camp, Tauber would invariably send several, sometimes dozens of girls to *Block* 25. He would pull out several rows of prisoners at random from marching *Kommandos* and send them away without even glancing at them. Now he is here.

They let us in one by one. In the next hall, near the door, stands a German doctor, Klein, then Tauber, and then the camp secretary Katia Singer,[28] who was writing down the prisoners' numbers. Part of the hall is divided by a rope. Behind the rope are those selected for *Block* 25.

---

27  The process of choosing who would die from those who were (temporarily) allowed to live.

28  She was a Slovakian Jewish prisoner.

Tensely, we watch the goings-on from afar. Each girl has to approach the doctor and turn around. Depending on Klein's decision, they then go to the right – to death – or to the left – to life.

Many who had been approved by the doctor are stopped again by the waiting Tauber. Some fall at his feet, crawling in despair and begging for pity. His arms crossed across his chest, he bursts out laughing. With his little finger, he signals an aide from the sauna and gives orders to pull away the unfortunate. She disappears in the crowd of her companions in adversity. After her, another one, and another. To the left, to the right.

*What are they looking for?* we ask each other.

*For boils, for scabies, for swollen feet,* someone whispers.

*This is the end of me,* whispers one.

*Look! Look at me! Am I badly scratched?* asks a girl standing near me. Her whole back is covered with black crusts of dried blood.

*No. Not too bad,* I try to reassure her.

We show each other our jagged backs, our swollen feet. We lie to each other. We try to reassure ourselves. We believe each other.

After all, everyone can see for themselves the wasted bodies, their pimples and boils. But when somebody reassures you that you're really not too bad, you believe and begin to compare yourself with others. It's comforting to find someone who looks worse than you do.

Our mutual inspection is briefly interrupted. Tauber savagely drags a woman along the ground. He kicks her, hard, with his sharp boots, splits her open. Blood spurts, the woman screams, and then there is silence. The honourable audience of gathered SS women and men enjoy and laugh at this curious spectacle. The murderer, arms crossed, waits for another victim.

He is tall, thin, his head like a poppy-head. His little eyes seem to penetrate our very insides. Nothing escapes him, not the tiniest movement. He is the true embodiment of a devil. It was well known that, though you might succeed in weaseling out of some selections, it was out of the question with Tauber present. His eyes were everywhere. We were convinced that Tauber could see what was going on behind his back.

Estusia and I hold each other's hands tightly. The rows in front of us are thinning out. Our turn. My heart pounds like a hammer. I straighten out as much as I can. I approach with a sure step. I turn around and wait.

In this moment, my fate will be decided. I stand and, with all the will power I can muster, try to control the nervous trembling that is invading me from top to bottom. I am terrified that he will hear the pounding of my heart. I don't know if this moment lasted for more than one or two seconds. For me it was a lifetime.

*To the left.*

Like a robot, I walk by Tauber, expecting to be turned back or kicked. Nothing.

I join the lucky few and tensely wait for my sister. She makes it through. We breathe a sigh of relief, kiss and embrace each other heartily. They dispense clothing. Here awaits a pleasant surprise. We are given decent dresses. But alas, how we looked in these dresses! Some are too large and long, some too tight and short. They cover our shapeless bodies comically. We look like rag dolls made by the clumsy hand of a young child. So what? We have our own clean dresses. We admire ourselves, making fun of ourselves in our comic apparel, totally forgetting about what we went through just a few moments ago, not paying attention to our unfortunate comrades behind the rope, averting our eyes from their jealous gaze.

We leave the sauna and enter our new camp. Just as in the other one, there are barracks on both sides of the camp's main street. The first *Block* on the right-hand side is the sauna, on the left, the kitchen. In the sauna, a few men remained, since they were waiting for a new sauna in the men's camp to open.

We march along the main street, turn onto the second path on the left. *Block* 11. Here we stop. The *Blockhova* and the secretary take down our numbers and we go in. We stand, dazzled. Running the entire length of the *Block* stretches a tiled brick furnace on which one could sit and warm oneself.

To the left and right of the furnace are wooden bunk beds, stacked three high. Real beds, not the stinking brick *Koja* where one felt as if buried alive in old Roman catacombs. These are real beds![29] They are narrow and hard, it is true, but beds all the same, where one can sleep all by oneself, or at the most two per bed. Here is something one can call one's very own, something pleasant, a place where one can rest a bit in the evening after a long hard day. One can stretch one's weary bones, stretch out as far as one desires, without fear of kicking somebody or of somebody kicking you.

The *Block* was well situated. Across from the camp entrance was the men's sauna; a little farther on, the *Brotkammer*. On the right, *Block* 10, which housed German *Kapos* and supervisors. On the left, *Block* 11, which housed the parcel post workers, members of the orchestra,[30] and now us.

---

29  We were in the wooden barracks that were usually assigned to non-Jews.

30  Beginning in 1941, a number of orchestras, including a women's orchestra were created in the Auschwitz-Birkenau camp complex. They were employed to facilitate the marching and counting of inmates and to entertain SS camp officials.

The area around the parcel post office and *Brotkammer* was very convenient from the point of view of "organizing,"[31] not so much for my sister and me, but for those shrewd girls who succeeded in insinuating themselves as helpers around the post and *Brotkammer*. This guaranteed that they would be the first and only ones to help themselves to crumbs and edible garbage, and so stave off the hunger, which meant the difference between life and death.

Not feeling the pangs of hunger and not facing constant torment, one became a different human being. An additional factor was that the body became used to its daily dose of bromide and didn't react to it any more. My thoughts ceased to concentrate exclusively on food and started to move into wider orbits and in different directions. Our lives seemed to improve.

Unfortunately, it was only the beginning. Shortly after we arrived at our new *Block*, Estusia fell ill. Typhus. She lost her appetite, burned with a high fever, and had no strength to stand or walk. She was falling off her feet. I couldn't leave her in the *Block*. I had to drag her to work. Weak myself, I don't know where I found the strength to get her to work and back. She begged for something spicy, something tasty, but I had nothing to give her. My heart broke when I looked at her pale face and wasting figure, when I heard her begging but couldn't help her.

There was nobody who could help, nobody who could advise me what to do for her. I was still such a child.[32] I had no idea how to take care of her. I sobbed loudly as I changed rags soaked in cold water to cool her forehead. Her fever dried the rags in no time.

Sometimes at night, I ran blindly with our bread rations in my hands and tried to barter them in *Kanada* for a piece of sugar or an apple.[33] The girls in *Kanada* had everything. And when sometimes I succeeded and brought these things to my sister, she weakly smiled her thanks. She didn't have the strength to speak.

There was a sort of "hospital" called the *Revier* in the old camp.[34] It provided little medical help; nobody cared for the sick. But at least those in the *Revier* did not have to stand at *Appel*, did not have to work, and so could rest during the day. However, there was a selection at the *Revier* every other day, after which only a few of the "patients" would be left. I couldn't take her there. I knew that even if I couldn't help her at all, at least we were together. That meant a lot.

---

31  Pilfering.

32  This was 1943, when I was fifteen years old.

33  We were allowed to wander between the barracks after work.

34  *Lager A.*

One night, Estusia lost consciousness. She called for our daddy, she asked where were we travelling. She breathed shallow, quick breaths. Everyone around us slept. I could hear the trucks going in the direction of the crematoria. I heard the terrible screams of victims being murdered and of little children calling for their mommies. Driven to despair, I sat near my unconscious sister. The screams outside and the noise of the trucks as they returned empty were driving me mad.

I didn't cry. My eyes burned and I felt stones in my throat and my heart. Something screamed within me: *Why? Why are they going there without resistance? Why am I sitting here next to my sister, looking at her suffering and being so totally helpless?*

And here was born in me a feeling to this point unknown. For the first time, my brain produced the clear thought of mutiny – *We shall not give in.* At that moment, I did not know how, I concentrated on this one thought with all my willpower.

With pursed lips, I changed the cold compresses. After a while, I noticed that her breathing had become calmer and that she had fallen asleep. I knew that she had passed the crisis. A silent sigh of relief escaped my breast. *She is saved!*

Slowly, Estusia recovered. She began to smile and had a terrific appetite. I sneaked her my ration of bread, pretending that I had gotten it "here and there." I did not feel hungry. I was too ecstatic to be hungry as I watched her coming back to life. That was enough nourishment for me.

Since the factory in which we were supposed to work wasn't ready yet, we were kept busy emptying the filthy slime from the ditches surrounding the camp. In the camp's terms, this was not considered hard labour. While I watched to see if anybody was approaching, Estusia could sit and rest for a while. The side where we were working bordered the crematorium. As we worked, we could see the goings-on there.

Prisoners in the *Sonderkommando*[35] worked in the crematorium, people devoid of any kind of feeling, their hearts changed to stone, feeling nothing. Every one of them had a girl in the camp that they helped. Working there by the crematorium, we could see how the men of the *Sonderkommando* approached the wires and flirted with the girls. They exchanged love letters with the girls that contained both obscene jokes and pathos. Many of the girls were illiterate and had to have somebody read these letters to them. Anyway, the girls weren't really that interested in the letters themselves, but in the parcels from the *Sonderkommando* that accompanied the letters.

---

35 Special work squad, usually workers in the crematoria.

With help or by themselves, they wrote back to their lovers, demanding chocolate, cakes, and other luxury items. In answer, the letters promised that as soon as a new transport arrived, they would have their wish.

Thus, the *Sonderkommando* awaited the transports. They wanted the transports to come so that they could send wonderful parcels to their lovers, to pilfer gold, to get drunk. I stood on the side, watching it all, my insides twisted with hunger, loathing these beasts in human forms.

The factory began to become a reality. We were transferred to another *Block*, this time *Block* 8. At first, there was no work. We stood on *Appel* for hours. The hard wooden clogs scratched my feet so painfully that I couldn't wear them and stood barefoot. It was terribly cold, a penetrating cold. I didn't have a sweater because I didn't know how to push and fight to get one. Others had two or three. My feet and hands were numb with cold. I couldn't move them.

When the whistles finally announced *Abtreten*, after a long *Appel,* they wouldn't let us inside the *Block*. They were cleaning. We stood by the walls, huddled together for warmth. More than one fainted from exhaustion and hunger, more than one was taken to the *Revier* with pneumonia, never to return.

As we stood like this, shivering and huddling, the *Lagerälteste* would appear and chase us to work, beating us with a riding crop. We ran and scattered all over the camp. Whoever could, hid, and didn't have to go to work. I don't know how it happened, but our *Blockhova* took a liking to my sister and made her a *Türwache*, a door-watchman, whose function was literally to watch the door to make sure that nobody got in or out during curfew, to warn if guards were approaching on unexpected visits, and so on.

Estusia's new job was a tremendous plus for us. First, we didn't have to stand and freeze so long at *Appel*. Second, Estusia started to receive more to eat. More soup, more extras like margarine or jam, sometimes even more bread. Our lot seemed to improve.

One day, they began pouring a new cement floor in our *Block*. We could not sleep in the *Stube* while the new floor was poured, because it would have left marks on the fresh cement. One girl, forgetting, stepped onto the fresh floor and left a mark. Unfortunately, our *Blockhova* caught her. She beat her terribly and took her to the *Lagerälteste*, complaining that the girl was insubordinate. The *Blockhova* demanded that the girl be punished. The *Lagerälteste* ordered the girl to *Block* 25. Thus, our *Blockhova*, guided by her ambition to have the most beautiful *Block,* and eager to show herself as a faithful and obedient servant to the Germans, sent a girl to her death for nothing at all.

I started to get sick. Countless pus-filled abscesses, tiny ones and big ones, appeared all over my body, especially on my backside. When I sat down, they would burst, and the pus would spill out and stick to my panties, spreading the infection. To get up, I first had to tear my underpants away from my skin, sobbing and screaming from pain. I couldn't stand it. It was draining away all of my strength and energy. One abscess after another, one near the other, merging into one big rotting mess.

I felt that I was rotting away. There was no ointment, no bandage, nothing. One day, there was a curfew. Selection! I froze. I knew this would be the end of me. There was no way of getting through a selection with a body like mine. But I didn't despair. I told myself that whatever happens, I am not going. Let them kill me. Here on the spot. I am not going.

The commission this time consists of *Lagerälteste*[36] Leo, *Lagerarzt*[37] Klein, and *Lagerkommandant*[38] Hoessler. They go from *Block* to *Block*. Slowly, they near our *Block*. I am strangely calm. Some kind of a deathly calm overtakes me. They are here.

*Alle raus!*[39]

They drive us out to one side of the courtyard.

The *Shtubhova*, linking hands, form a human chain. They let each girl through one at a time. Among the girls is my sister. Poor Estusia. I can see how pale she is, how much she is terrified for me. Everyone has to undress completely and parade naked in front of the commission.

*Shoes and stockings off!* yells the *Lagerälteste*, hitting all those nearby who are wearing shoes. Though a prisoner herself, the *Lagerälteste*, was the worst of all three of them.

Slowly, calmly, I undress. I leave on my panties, stockings, and shoes. I look on as the girls follow one another. One pimple, one scratch, and they are being stood off on the side. I smile cynically and look at those whom I shall soon join. I look at my sister for a long, long time. Who knows, maybe it is for the last time. I am not worried for myself, but I am sorry for her; she will suffer so.

Finally, I step forward. With my head high, completely calm, I wait for the *Lagerälteste* to hit me, to order me to take off my stockings and shoes, and then to join the group of the condemned.

---

36 "Director" of the camp. He was a prisoner who carried out the orders of the *Lagerkommandant*.

37 Camp doctor.

38 Camp commandant.

39 "Everybody out!"

Nothing. The doctor pats me on my shoulder and waves me on. I cringe and look at him, as at a madman. But there is no time to think. The *Lagerälteste* pulls at me and I go through. I don't think that I am superstitious. I don't believe in miracles, but this time I was overwhelmed by an indescribable feeling. To this day, I cannot explain what happened on that day. I felt guilty. *Why me? Why was I left alive, when others who looked better than me were sent to their deaths?*

Life went on. There were huge transports from Poland, Greece, and Belgium, but nobody from the transports came into the camp. Standing by the wires, we could see women and children, young and old, all so very tired, walking in masses, not knowing where. At the gates of the camp, the orchestra played polkas, mazurkas, and other gay melodies, playing for those going to their death. Shattered, we would return to our *Block*.

One day, Estusia and I got into a conversation with the *Block* secretary[40] and Marta, the girl who was in charge of distributing bread. We talked about the situation of Jews in Europe, and about the situation of Jews in the camp.

Among others, they told us about the group of people from the first transport of Slovakian Jews, who when chosen as the first *Sonderkommando* refused *en masse* and were all murdered.

They were to assist in the process of gassing people and to work in the crematoria burning the bodies of the victims. They refused, knowing full well that refusal would be punished by death. Such a heroic act and so little known!

Those heroes chose between two kinds of death and chose to die in defiance rather than to collaborate with the barbarians. Unfortunately, not everybody followed their example.

I reacted by saying that if we all united together and wouldn't go like sheep to the slaughter, we, too, could achieve something. After all, there were so many of us and so few of them. Anyway, as far as I was concerned, I was not going to go quietly.

They laughed at me and said: *There were people smarter than you, and they went too.*

But I did not accept this argument. After this conversation, we started to get closer and friendship developed.

We finally started work in the factory. A new era of camp life was beginning. Of course, prior to work, we had to go through the sauna. Here we got brand new clothes – blue and gray striped dresses, and aprons and

---

40 Her job was to keep track of how many prisoners were working in which *Kommando.*

jackets made from the same material as the dresses. Actually, it was recycled paper, a metaphor for cloth. It was very coarse, mercilessly scratching the skin.

Still, it was one of the most elegant outfits in the camp, usually out of reach of the Jewish girls. We got it as an exception, as our *Kommando* had now attained a place of prominence in the camp hierarchy. Of course, it was also to make a good impression on the civilian world, which shortly we would meet at work.

Before starting work, we had to go through strict training. I think, *What will happen to us if they discover that we are not metallurgists, that I have no idea what a metallurgist does?* But one mustn't show those fears! I put a good face on a bad business and cautiously look around. Maybe I can learn something from the others.

*Listen,* I say to the one nearest me, *have you ever worked in a metal factory?*

*Who, me? Of course! What do you think?,* she answers.

*What machine did you operate?,* I insist.

*Hmm,* she says. *I will tell you a secret, but don't tell anybody. I have never worked in a factory before.*

Well, I feel much better. I ask another one and another and yet another. More or less all give me the same answer. One lies more convincingly than another; they are afraid to tell the truth because there are many spies around. The worst are the German Jewish girls.

A whole transport of them came directly from a munitions factory in Germany. Now they stand in little groups and complain bitterly that the Polish girls know nothing, that they will have to do our work, that they will be thrown out because of us, and so on.

Swine! They haven't even started yet but they are already full of fear, thinking only of themselves. Naturally, all the best jobs belong to them because, after all, they are Germans.

One of them, by mistake, turns to me and complains: *We will all be thrown out! Those ignorant Polish girls will compromise us.*

*Don't worry,* I tell her. *We shall teach them and they will be as good as us.* I answer with assurance as if I have spent my whole life in a munitions factory.

*What?,* she exclaims, *We have to show them!?*

*You don't want to, well, then go to the guard and complain. I am Polish too.*

Angrily, I turn my back to her and begin to admire my new outfit – a slip and panties, clean, too. The panties have a red ribbon instead of an elastic. Never mind, I make a beautiful bow and walk on to get a sweater.

There are still a few girls in front of me. While waiting, I observe the girls who work in the sauna, who at this moment are distributing our clothes. In front of them are piles of neatly folded underwear, dresses, sweaters and, further on, shoes.

Quickly, quickly they distribute everything, without once lifting their eyes to see what they give to whom. They are completely absorbed in sorting out the clothes. They throw into our faces all the rags, torn, dirty, good for nothing. They put aside for themselves what looks in good shape and is pretty.

Now a young girl stands in front of them, petite, thin, a child. She stands in her underwear, much too large for her, shivering with cold, her teeth chattering. It is winter and frost is fast approaching. They throw a sleeveless rag at her. The child's eyes fill with tears and she begs, she is so cold, she doesn't want anything prettier but if only it had sleeves...?

*What!,* bellows the other, *What! So you think that you are in a store? That you can choose what you want? What? I will show you a store!* The witch hits the girl in the face so hard that the little one falls.

*What!,* screams the witch, *You're trying to be funny? Over to the guard!*

She drags the girl along the ground to the uniformed guard, complaining that the girl refused to accept what she was given, that she is stopping the work and creating disorder. The woman guard kicks the unfortunate girl and hits her with her riding crop, leaving bluish-red stripes on her trembling body.

The informer returns to her work triumphantly and continues to put aside heavy warm sweaters for herself and her friends, rags for us. I thought that I would suffocate. *She has it so warm and clean here in the sauna. She has as much hot water as she wants. She is never hungry. What right does she have to deprive this poor child of a sweater with sleeves? Who gives her the right to lift her hand and denounce the girl to the guard? What kind of conscience does she have to rob us of what the Germans give us?*

I am so naive. Where am I looking for conscience? Conscience is a commodity, a luxury, found in a free world but not here in Auschwitz. What does she need a conscience for, so that she can freeze and be hungry? That she pays for it with her life? She couldn't care less. All that matters to her is that she lives. Yes, she is well, she no longer knows what feelings are, she no longer understands pain. I know. And how envious I am of her. I loathe her, I hate her, but I envy her.

Why can't I close my eyes to everything that is going on around me? Instead, it is just the opposite. I see it all, and I feel it all, and there is absolutely nothing I can do to help. *Why? What for? Why do I see it all?*

We return to the *Block* and again stand for long hours on *Appel*. Again I have long tiring hours of nightmares. I lie down and before my eyes appear row upon row of people, frozen, debilitated, little children falling asleep in their mothers' numb arms, men with bruised faces, apprehensive, terrified. They stand, they move slowly on swerving knees, step after step after step, dreaming of respite in this house[41] with its tall chimney, gushing fire and black smoke, slowly, quietly, by the hundreds upon hundreds, by the thousands upon thousands. *Yes, you wretches, you will find peace there, forever.* I wake up with a start.

I want to run, to shout, *This camp is an illusion, this orchestra a lie! You are being taken to your deaths!* But tall electrified wires separate me from them. The muzzles of machine guns gape at me from guard towers situated every few yards all around the perimeter of the wires. I hear the quiet growling of the dogs. Their white fangs, glistening in the darkness, warn me that the camp guards don't sleep, that their masters are watching. Those people there behind the wires wouldn't believe me anyway, just as I didn't believe those who told me when I first arrived that I no longer had parents.

So I lie down again. I hear truck after truck. I hear the screams of murdered victims. I laugh and laugh. For I no longer see people. I no longer see flames escaping from the chimney. It is not a flame, it is a whole golden loaf of bread, just for me, for my sister and me. Ah, the bread disappears, there are machines all around me. Wherever I turn there are machines. I want to run away but the machines roar, clamour and whistle, whistle, whistle.

*Aufstehen! Aufstehen!*[42]

I wake up covered with sweat. Instead of machines, there are beds everywhere. Instead of a loaf of bread, there is a gnawing pain at the pit of my stomach. This is no longer a dream, but sad, naked truth. Suddenly, I remember that today we start work in the factory. I jump up and get dressed quickly. I grab the piece of rag torn from my slip that serves as my sheet at night and as both my towel and tablecloth during the day. It is the deep of the night. My eyes are still glued shut with sleep. In spite of my desperate rubbing, they keep closing by themselves.

I walk blindly, stumbling with each step. I near the door. I don't see it yet, but I can feel the cold draft. With delight, I breathe in the refreshing air. But once outside I can't help shivering. The cold shakes me like jelly. Brrr! I retreat, but the awful stink that you don't smell as much when you are inside pushes me forward. It is still dark. There is only the weak light from the lamps on the wires, illuminating a stingy little piece of ground,

---

41  From a distance, the crematoria looked like houses with unnaturally large chimneys.

42  "Get up! Get up!"

the ditch surrounding the camp, and the double rows of electrified wire. A little higher up are the guard booths from where you could hear whistling, boots stomping, and, from time to time, shooting. This is how the guards amused themselves and shortened their boring guard duty. Each shot reverberated, making thousands of little echoes that trembled in the air and disappeared far away in the free world.

But nobody heard it there, all were buried in a stony sleep. We, like sleeping beauties, waited for a Prince Charming to rescue us. But our Prince Charming made us wait for a long, long time. In the meantime, a wicked sorcerer lorded it over the camp, holding everything in his grip of fire and gas.

Now, in the middle of the night, a black banner of smoke bursts into the sky, interrupted from time to time by leaping flames, the souls of murdered victims. Where did these souls float? Nothing is lost in nature. There, even higher than the chimney, stretched the navy blue sky, studded with stars. What are stars? Maybe those are the flown-away souls. They twinkle at us so pleasantly, so encouragingly, giving us heart and sympathy as if wishing to help. At least something beckons.

I smile at them and run to the *Waschraum*.[43] In front of the door, everybody pushes to be first.

Everything is seething as dozens of women crowd the door, pushing, stepping on each other. At the door stands the one responsible for the building, a thick stick in her hand, hitting whomever she can reach. Blood flows. The hurt and beaten scream and sob.

Somebody yells to let in a girl who had fainted. In answer, a bucket of icy water is poured over her. Thus revived, she goes away, trembling, cold teeth rattling, water dripping all over her. Since there is nothing to dry herself with, no change of clothes, she will have to stand all wet for the long *Appel*. She will develop pneumonia. Then the *Revier* and the end.

Others turn away, bruised, battered. It takes many weeks for the skin to heal. There is a washroom, but you can't wash. So a little scratch gets easily infected, turning into a pus-filled wound, making you a prime subject for selection. We are filthy. The lice eat us alive.

Our *Blockhova* inspects our clogs. If our clogs are dirty, she grabs us by the hair, beats us, kicks us, and then makes us kneel for a long time in sand full of sharp pebbles, our hands in the air. The *Blockhova*, maybe eighteen years old or twenty at the most, abuses the older women, dragging them along the ground. We are not let into the washroom. When it rained,

---

43 Bathhouse.

you could clean your clogs in a puddle; otherwise, you had to spit on them and clean them with a piece of paper or a rag. But where can we find paper? There is no paper, so a hand will do. We can be filthy and vermin-eaten as long as our clogs look clean.

*Well, in a crowd it will pass,* I think to myself, looking critically at my clogs. I return to the *Block.* A battle rages. They have just brought drum-like kettles full of a stinking beverage called "tea." Near the kettles, a real war rages. There is pushing and fighting as everybody stretches out her cup, trying to scoop up some liquid. The kettles overturn from all the pushing. The entire contents spill on the ground. Now the scooping begins – right from the ground, with bare hands.

Greedily, quickly, they gather the filthy drink from the ground and, overjoyed with their treasure, bring it to their less fortunate comrades. Is it a wonder that we die like flies of diarrhea? Is it a wonder that hundreds die of typhus? Is it surprising that, being so weak, with no resistance, they greet death as deliverance?

Dawn approaches slowly. We stand on *Appel* for a very long time. I twist my neck and look at the sky. The stars vanish one after another. It is so strange. There is still one glittering. Shivering, I can see it clearly. Suddenly it goes out and there is nothing. I strain my eyes in vain. I can't even find the place where the star used to be. It is the same as with all of the other stars.

*Just like us,* I think, *we also wink out one after another.* How many similarities there are between nature and our daily gray existence! Here, too, life burns and goes out and there is a day following night. Is there going to be a day after our night? Are we going to live to see it?

*Yeah, here,* laughs the tall chimney cynically.

*Here,* strum the long rows of wires ironically.

*Here,* shouts the green uniform, a lash in its hand, a dog at its side.

From the stars I fall back to earth. Inconspicuously it becomes light. My feet and the palms of my hands are numb with the cold. I can't move them even to warm myself because the tiniest movement causes tremendous pain. *What will this day bring?,* I think to myself.

Today, we are going to work for the first time. Ah, never mind, I don't want to think about it. Let the *Appel* finish already. Finally, the longed-for *Abtreten.* But today we do not return to the *Block,* but rather approach the gates, in rows of five, and range ourselves among the other working *Kommandos.*

The columns march, following each other in rows of five, marching to the rhythm of the orchestra, marching straight, like strings at attention. *Left, left, left,* all marching to the rhythm with the same foot, not daring to turn around for a split second.

Our masters stand at the gates, looking at us critically, sadistic smiles on their faces. Rigid with terror, we go slowly, thousands of people enslaved to work against ourselves, contributing to the victory of Satan.

We march. *Left, left, left.* My heart pounds. *Now they will slap me for sure, maybe my kerchief is crooked, maybe I am not holding my arm the way I should, maybe I am not in line with the rest of my row?*

I see their bestial faces as through a mist as we pass by. They have the faces of criminals. Here the criminals are the jailers and the innocent are the prisoners, waiting to be executed. The *Lagerkommandant,* the *Oberaufseherin,* the *Arbeitsdienstführer,*[44] all of them stand in wait for a victim – the smallest, the thinnest, the weakest, those who stumble. One wave of a finger, one look, and one of the girls is taken out to *Block* 25.

The orchestra plays a march and we march to the rhythm, *Left, left, left.* We march, march like the well-oiled wheels of a machine, all looking alike, indistinguishable. Only our numbers are different. Numbers, not human beings are marching.

We hold our bowls in our right hand, our clogs in our left. The sharp gravel pierces our feet, blue, and frozen from standing so long on *Appel.* Finally, with relief, we pass the gate. Now we pass by the guards standing with their dogs, a whole pack of two-legged and four-legged dogs. The four-legged ones, their eyes bloodshot, foam on their muzzles, whining and straining at the taut leashes, are impatient for the command to bury their fangs in living flesh. Involuntarily, I tremble.

It is long ago since we passed by the guards. It is long ago since the sound of the orchestra vanished. It is long ago since the long rows of camp wires and guard booths vanished from the horizon. Yet I can't shake off the image of bloodshot, whining, bloodthirsty beasts. Why? Can the dogs differentiate between Jews and non-Jews? Are we really so bad, so threatening that the whole of nature has turned against us?

We walk for so long that my feet are swollen, burning, my heart pounds. I am covered with sweat. Yet there is no sign of the end of our walk. I see people around me beginning to slow, breathing heavily, the neat rows unraveling. A swish of a lash tears through the air, a German curse follows. With their remaining strength, the rows straighten out again.

We pass by the fields in which our comrades work. We pass by roads constructed with our own hands. We pass by male prisoners carrying heavy loads of dirt and rock. The beautiful roads twist between green manicured

---

44  Chief of work assignments.

lawns, the fields extend far out toward the horizon, seeded with all kinds of vegetables and wheat. All this is our work, our blood, our sweat. All this labour, under constant threat of the lash, without a second of respite, without a drop of water in the hottest weather, without a spoonful of warm food on the coldest days.

We are still walking. The road, straight up to now, forks to the right and left. On the left is the free world. Mothers stand hugging their babies, the men probably at work or in the army, young boys replacing them. The children stand, pointing their fingers at us – how nicely we walk, how we all wear the same clothes, how nicely we sing.

They ask their mothers, *Who are they?*

And the mothers say, *They are bad people, very bad people, the worst people in the world. They are Jews.*

*Worse than thieves?,* ask the children.

*Worse!*

*Worse than bandits?*

*Worse!*

And in their little brains, a concept builds – *the worst people in the world are the Jews*. But why is a Jew so bad? What did they do? This, neither the child nor his mother knew, neither the guard nor the dog walking beside them. Forcibly torn from my mother's arms, from the warmth of my home, torn from my toys and books in my nursery, I ask myself the same question. Does the child over there mean *me*? Or my mistreated companions?

Finally, we reach our goal, a building, clothed in smooth red walls, with no windows, just some skylights on the roof. The building's roof looks as if the peaked roofs of smaller structures had been merged, like a series of triangular slabs joined together. Their bases are covered with dark blue paint. Just as in the camp, tall rows of wires and a large gate surround the building.

We line up in the courtyard and wait to see what will happen next.

Two civilians come away out from the factory and look us over. With sceptical smiles, they go through the rows, smirking at each other. Both are portly, well fed, their thick necks suffused red. With their hands stuck in their pockets, they choose the tallest and heaviest from among us.

*I am sure that they will return us to the camp,* I think to myself anxiously. What was I afraid of? I don't know. Somehow, this droning factory attracted me. It had something of freedom in it, something that distanced us from the camp and that enabled us to hide for a while from the spectre of the chimney. That was already something. But most important of all, working in the Union,[45] we were no longer subject to selections.

One, two, three groups of girls disappear inside the factory. I move forward with a few others. When the two chiefs look at me, I feel my face flush. All of this is so new and wonderful. All at once, my new wooden clogs that I was so proud of just a few minutes ago, my new striped blue and gray dress, so carefully pressed all night long under the mattress, my shiny white kerchief covering my one and a half centimetres of newly grown hair – how terribly shabby they all have become. If I could have, I would have sunk beneath the ground.

It lasts but a moment. We pass by them and go inside the factory. Immediately, we are engulfed by the roar and rattle of the machinery. Everything vibrates to the rhythm of the hot machines. The air is full of a strange yellow dust with an acrid smell. It nauseates us. I feel weak. I feel as if all these as-yet-unseen machines are pounding inside my head. Hot and cold currents run all through my body.

With all the control in my possession, I refuse to give in to the impulse to stop for just a minute. Eyes closed, I continue walking with my comrades. When I open my eyes, I see that there are seven of us.

We are led along a long wide corridor. On the right of this corridor, behind a dividing wall, were an office, showers, and a cloakroom. On the left, through stretched mesh, we could see girls working at long tables. Further in, there was more mesh through which could be heard the roar of the machines.

The corridor widened at one end. On the left was a high glass wall. A door in the middle replaced the wire mesh. A little further, on a little elevation, were two glass cages that constituted the *Meisters'*[46] offices. They were built in such a way that a *Meister* standing in his office had a clear view of the entire factory and could observe everything.

Behind the office, the corridor turned left. Here were the last and most interesting departments of the factory, called the *Montage*.[47] All the component pieces were put together in the *Montage*, the pieces that had been manufactured and checked carefully by many hands, both those of the prisoners and of their German foremen. On one side of the *Montage* was a storage area at the end of the corridor; on the other, a loading area.

---

45  Weichsell Metall Union Werke. This plant produced rockets and munitions, among which were shell fuses.

46  Civilians whose job was quality control.

47  The assembly line.

Behind the *Montage* was the *Laufband*,[48] the *Spritzraum*,[49] and the *Packerei*, respectively.[50]

The factory's prospectus advertised bicycles. But, as we learned later, they were manufacturing munitions. AZ1 and AZ23[51] – from here they were shipped to another factory to be further integrated and assembled.

We are led to the big door in the glass wall. As we walk in, the first thing that meets our eyes is a large white board suspended from one of the beams supporting the slanting roof. On the board, is a big number 10.

Our nostrils are hit with a sharp acrid smell and by the yellow dust floating in the air. A heavy yellow layer of dust covers everything in the room. The dust irritates my throat. I want to cough but can't. I sit on one of the stools that are arranged on both sides of a long table.

The table was situated about one metre from the door. My back was to the glass wall separating us from the *Montage*. There was a half-metre space between the wall and me. This space was one of the first things that I noticed. I laughed to myself. *What stupidity! Couldn't they move the tables another half metre so they would be closer to the wall?*

Soon enough, I understood why I was the stupid one. Not only were we surrounded by clear glass walls on all sides, not only was our every move, our every look spied upon by dozens of eyes, but behind every table, every machine, was a space where those watching us could walk behind our backs in the hope of catching us at some offence.

Every table had a German prisoner–supervisor, every department a German prisoner *Kapo*. Each department was separated from another by glass walls so that, standing in one department, one could see through to the next one; of course, that is why they were made of glass. To be watched constantly by many pairs of spying eyes was a terrible feeling, to sit and not be able to turn around to determine from which direction the spying eyes were watching us.

Everywhere and at all times, we were under the ever-watching eyes. How often we heard the word, *Kontrollen!*[52] We would shudder. Some girls had a few cigarettes, others maybe a letter. We were paralyzed with

---

48  Conveyor belt.

49  Stenciling room.

50  The packing and shipping room.

51  These were the numbers stenciled on the boxes of munitions.

52  Search or inspection.

fear even if we had nothing. We never knew when the *Kontrolle* would descend upon us: usually when we least expected it.

The searches were actually intended to make sure the prisoners did not possess articles from the free world, anything that might have indicated contact between the civilians and the prisoners. But our *Kapos* robbed us of all the possessions that we had collected with such great difficulty, such as little boxes, pieces of material, pocket knives, precious pieces of soap, and other necessary articles of daily living. We had to start all over again.

There was strict punishment for sabotage. Eating during work was considered to be "sabotage." We could go to the toilet only at specified times. Conversations with the men were strictly forbidden. There were a whole range of other prohibitions.

I sit and look around. Near me are many others. I don't know who they are. There are two on each side of me, then another two, and four across the table. That makes eleven of us. But nobody is interested in her neighbour. Everyone is lost in her own thoughts. I think that most of them are quite worried, just as I am, that we will soon be given our work, and it will then become quite clear how ignorant we are. Well, whatever will be, will be.

I continue looking around. Just across is a small room. Actually, the "room" consists of two glass walls hugging a corner of the big hall. On the door is a little sign: *Ambulanz.*[53] The doors are slightly open and I can see inside. There is a little table with a bottle on it, probably iodine, a few rolls of paper bandage. In the middle is a wastepaper basket and one chair. This is the *Ambulanz.*

Next to the *Ambulanz* are heavy machinery called *Presse.*[54] The *Presse* are giant machines, one next to the other just across from where we sit, facing us and hiding the department behind them. Every three minutes, they spit out this awful yellow dust at our faces. Every three minutes, I see two arms – blue-veined, tense, stretched out, lifting with difficulty the heavy pistons of the *Presse.* And then, a short time later, two hands in thin dirty gloves sort out little pieces called *Einsatzstücke*[55] from the hot mass. Then the same hands clean off the machine with a vacuum blower hose. The hose raises clouds of the yellow dust and sends little bits of the hot plastic material flying.

Quickly the machine is filled with a new mass and the piston comes down again for three minutes. Then I see a red face bathed in running

---

53  First-aid station.

54  Stamping presses.

55  Insert-pieces.

rivulets of sweat, two sunken eyes eaten by dust, pain, and starvation, black lips cracked with fever. I hear a dry, deep cough. The piston rises again and the same hands and the same dust and the same face.

Until once when the piston lifted and didn't descend again. On the floor there lay a man.

A man? No. A number. Number 141,293. A doctor came, or rather somebody who performed the function of a doctor. He had a cup of cloudy water, which he emptied on the fallen creature. Nothing. The doctor knelt down and hit the man in the face. "The number" opened his eyes. In the meantime, the *Meister* was called. Herr Strepfel himself deigned to come.

The sick man, roused to consciousness by a stiff kick, opened his eyes again. The *Meister* wanted to make sure that the man was not faking. His fate was sealed when, after a kick that might have woken a corpse, a small stream of blood dripped slowly from his mouth.

*Scabby Jew!* screamed the Meister, *I will teach you to sabotage! Off to the crematorium! All of you who think of sabotage will follow him! Off, now, back to work! I will show you!*

The *Meister* walked off, looking around for somebody to operate the machine. I cringed and bent over, pretending to be deep in my work. My neighbour on the right passed me the *Einsatzstücke*.

In front of each one of us was a different little precision measuring instrument called a *Lehre*[56] to check the accuracy of the indentations in the *Einsatzstücke*. The work was passed very quickly from hand to hand. You couldn't stop or slow down, because a whole pile would form in front of you immediately, and it wouldn't take long for a heavy German paw to colour your cheeks red.

There was no question of cheating and letting a piece go by without measuring it, because it would show up immediately on the next machine on my left, and a sabotage report would follow. Sabotage report! We saw what it looked like. If you scratch – sabotage; if you turn your head – sabotage. Even the constant, monotonous whir of the *Presse* seemed to be droning, *Sa – bo – tage! Sa – bo – tage!*

*Quick! Quick! Let them see how diligently I am working!* One after another the little pieces move through my hands, my eyes look down at my *Lehre*. My hands move continuously. I can hardly feel them anymore. My back hurts from bending over.

*Work! Work! I mustn't stop.* I dare not let anyone see how tired I am. I bend over lower as if paying closer attention to my work. My hands

---

56  Gauge.

continue to move mechanically. Stealthily, I close my eyes. It lasts just a fraction of a second, and I lift my head.

*No, no, I shouldn't, I have to work.* Two separate beings are playing a tug of war inside me. To whom should I listen? Who is the real me? What am I? One whispers, *Work! Work! Work!* and the other tempts, *Sleep! Sleep! Sleep!*

And the first again – *Take care! Take care! Take care!*

And the second – *Nobody will see! Nobody will see! Nobody, Nobody!*

On the one hand, life; on the other, munitions. *Leave me alone! Get away from me! Why are you torturing me? What to do, give in to the tiredness? Put my head on the table? Yes, I can do it! But after?* I continue to work, even faster. *I can't contemplate the after! Fine, but nothing else awaits me anyway. Our fate is sealed, we just don't know how long we have. Why then continue to suffer, and lend our hands to making munitions?*

But something, hardly heard, whispers very quietly, *Maybe?* And this tiny hope, this tiny "maybe" tips the scales away from depression. Yes, it is because of this tiny "maybe" that we suffer and voluntarily prolong our hell.

I overcome my fatigue, I open my eyes as wide as I can and work. Before me, other hands measure the *Einsatzstücke*. The smallest indentations are carefully measured, every square millimetre. Nothing escapes our attention.

And then a number, *X*, the last link in our chain arranges the *Einsatzstücke* on a board in neat rows of a hundred and takes it to the *Montage*. She stops at the window and reports, *AZ23. Einsatzstücke hundert.*

The *Meister* stands in his office and watches everything, his thumbs hooked behind his suspenders. Yes, we work with the *Einsatzstücke*. We ourselves are *Einsatzstücke*, checked and measured.

Our *Einsatzstücke* are worked lovingly and intensively, are kept warm. Hundreds of people make sure that they are precise, shiny, whole.

And us? Who takes care of us? Who gives us minimal hygiene? Who warms us during the cold *Appels*? Who gives us food that we can't eat?

Ah, well, this is war! Arms and ammunition are more important than human cattle. Working flesh is available and plentiful. It doesn't cost anything. The old, the disabled, those whose life juices were sucked up by the machines, who were infected forever by the constant dust, filth, and bacteria, they are no longer needed. They receive their eternal leave. In their stead, ready in reserve, are multitudes of the young and strong.

*Einsatzstücke* have to be perfect at all times, a flawed one cannot be substituted by another one. This is why we must make sure that this expensive material doesn't go to waste. We have to give everything we have, our blood, our sweat, our strength. We are expendable. Should we waste the precious commodity, we pay with our heads. It is easy to lose one's head.

But ten others are waiting for each of our places. That is why we look tensely at each move of the tiny hand on the instrument's face. That is why the hand, sensitive to each tremble of the huge machine, lifted the piston without letting it drop.[57] That is why we competed with each other to gain the approval of our foreman, all the time trembling with fear lest we hear the dreaded word "discharge."

Our hands worked mechanically, repeating one and the same movement. We went mechanically at specified times to the toilet, to get our soup, when inevitably we would be beaten for pushing and pulling. I was becoming a robot.

The "machines" have a quota of pieces that have to be produced. They work without rest, sometimes even without a break for lunch. Woe to them should the machine develop a defect! They are lost. Should they lose five minutes, they will not be able to produce the quota demanded. This is considered sabotage.

The dust from the machines settled in our lungs. Our eyes strained from focusing constantly on one point. I felt weaker by the day, as the murderous dust slowly poisoned me through my pores.

I was still at my own seat, at my own work. But around me, many things changed. They increased production in the factory inversely with our declining strength: the daily quota of finished product grew from 1,500 to 3,000 *Einsatzstücke* at the same time our numbers fell to 100 out of the original 250. Five hundred new girls replaced the 150 who were gone.

I got to know my co-workers. Across from me at the press, a German woman prisoner replaced the dead man. On my right was a young woman, a Belgian Jew.

Very smart, once a teacher, now she was the image of wretchedness and despair. The conditions had broken her completely. She let herself go and paid no attention to herself. Terribly dirty, she provided a picnic ground for the lice who were eating her alive. She was scratching all the time. Her head was covered with a kerchief. Her glistening glasses were the only visible feature on her grimy face other than her nose, which dribbled snot onto the table. Wearing the striped prisoner's dress that was too thin for the Polish frost, she had caught a cold with a fever and had lost her appetite.

---

57 If it dropped, it would break. The process was not automated.

Since she couldn't eat, she was forever fumbling at her bread crumbs with her dirty hands. When they eventually got moldy she would give them to her friend. By not eating, she weakened her stomach and came down with dysentery. Often she would soil herself without noticing it. The horrible smell would betray her, and the other girls couldn't sit next to her. It was terrible. Poor girl, with a fever over forty degrees, she was dragging herself to work as long as she could. She was killing herself. Even worse, she was infecting others with dysentery, a terrible and contagious disease.

About half of us were stricken. We shared the bowls we used for eating. Eating from each other's bowls infected us all. Typhus, dysentery, malaria, and scabies were rampant. The dust-filled, closed air of the factory did not help either.

One day, the *Kapos* and the SS woman *Aufseherin*[58] went through the factory, listing the numbers of those that were thin and looked sick. Among those listed were many who were quite healthy, but nobody cared. The following day, 350 new prisoners came to work. Those listed were never seen again.

I got used to my work. It came easily by now. This gave me the opportunity to look around and get to know the secrets of the factory. Of course, it had to be done carefully, to preserve all the appearances of continuing to be hard at work.

Here is a suitable moment! There is a power failure.[59] No electricity for the machines means that our tables are empty. Ecstatic that we can straighten out our aching bones, we stretch at our stools and lean comfortably on the tables. We begin to chat a bit. There is plenty to gab about. At our table, we have an international gathering.

The first is Sheindle, from Warsaw. From left to right, Aneta, Greek; me; Roza, Belgian; Sala, Polish; Paula, German; Irene, Hungarian, and our supervisor, Basia, Polish. Luckily, we were all Jewish girls.

---

58  Overseer.

59  At first, there were intermittent power failures due to equipment overload. Later, in addition, the plant operations would also be stopped due to the threat of Allied bombing. On the latter occasions, the factory would stop and the air-raid sirens wail. We did not hear the planes. They must have been too high or too far away. The SS and German civilians would grab their gas masks and run into the air-raid shelter, probably leaving a skeleton staff or the *Kapos* in charge. We sat under our work tables, praying that the bombs would fall on us so that they would also destroy the factory and the Germans. They didn't. Once, the eerie silence in the factory was interrupted by the beautiful songs of the Greek Jews. The men's and women's voices joined in a haunting chorus across their physical separation. They sang, "Triana! Oh! Oh! Oh! le Triana!"

I look across at the German woman who operates the *Presse* opposite us. One can see the murderous toll the machine is taking on her. The Germans did not have their hair cut, nor did they have numbers tattooed on their arms. We envied them so. When she first arrived, she was a strong, healthy young woman. Her hair, long and shiny, was the subject of our jealousy. Now there are shadows under her eyes, wrinkles on her face. Her hair is matted, covered with yellow dust.

There is relative quiet in the hall. Since there is still no work at our table, I decide to be daring. I look around. I do not see anyone near, neither the hated yellow armband of the *Kapo* or the blue overalls of the foreman. I get up, my heart beating faster with excitement. I sit down again. No, I am not going.

But the machine irresistibly beckons to me. I have to see how it works. I get up and walk quickly to it. It is only a few steps, yet it came with such difficulty.

I stand there making faces at my companions, who don't quite yet comprehend what has happened. What is going on? I had gotten up from the table. This never happened before. They look at me as if they were seeing me for the first time in their lives.

I smile at them and look closer at her machine. There is a big circular form with seven circular holes. Using a little spoon, one fills each of these holes with yellow powder. Then the form is slid into the machine and the piston is lowered for three minutes.

The machine is set for a specific temperature. The combination of heat and pressure changes the powder into a solid material. Meanwhile another form is filled with powder. After three minutes, the piston rises.

Holding the finished pieces in one hand, the woman cleans the machine with a hose that she holds in her other hand. A sharp blast of hot air blows out all the tiniest leftover pieces and dust. Then a new form is put in and the piston is lowered, while the old form is cleaned and inspected for damage.

Sometimes, the pieces come out flawed because of slight changes in temperature. If the apparatus is too cold, the pieces burst; too hot and they come out full of blisters. These spoiled pieces were called *Ausschuss*[60] or *Ausschütten.*[61]

Standing and looking, I instinctively started to fill the little holes with the powder, using the small spoon. At the right moment, I wanted to lift

---

60  Rubbish, garbage.

61  To pour out.

the form and put it into the machine. I lifted it with both my hands but almost immediately let it go. It was very heavy.

The German woman looked at me and laughed. This laughter pricked my pride. I gathered all the strength I had and, turning half around, I succeeded in lifting the form and putting it in. I just stood there, red-faced.

At the same time, I thought, *Dear God, how can she do it all day long?* Having done it once, I was half-dead.

I didn't say it aloud, but the German, as if guessing my thoughts, said, *This is heavy work.*

*Yes, rather.* I tried to sound nonchalant.

I was a bit afraid. After all, she was a German. If she saw how hard it was for me, she could easily ask the foreman to put me on the machine. They would do things like that: if they took a dislike to somebody, they could cause them all kinds of unpleasantness. It was easier for them to order somebody else to work than to perform it themselves.

Themselves healthy, strong, and used to hard work, they would taunt us, *Jewish vermin! Lazy bitches! We shall teach you to work!*

The German workers toiled for their *Vaterland.*[62] *They* could put their hearts into their work. Most of them occupied important positions in the camp; many were *Kapos* and supervisors. They had black triangles in front of their numbers, denoting criminals and prostitutes.

The prostitutes were totally shameless. They gloated about their male conquests. They were in their own element, sleeping with male prisoners and SS men. They received wonderful things from their lovers, things like food, jewellery, clothes, which they couldn't possibly have had in the free world. They lacked nothing. All of it came from the Jewish transports. Bribed, the SS men turned a blind eye.

It is not surprising that those with black triangles felt much better being in the camp than in the free world, where all they could expect was to be hungry and to sit in bomb shelters. They were the ruling class in the camp and had no wish to leave the camp. They were very unhappy when notified that their sentences were up.

They had people subordinated to them, on whom they could vent all their rage and sadism with impunity. They were all-powerful and they abused us as much as they could. They would beat us constantly and complain to the authorities about us. With few exceptions, we were given the hardest jobs.

---

62  Fatherland.

In the toilets, where we were allowed to go en masse twice a day, at 9 a.m. and 5 p.m., they would pour cold water on us and chase us out with riding crops. We suffered a lot, not being able to satisfy our most basic physiological needs.

But not all of them were like that. There were exceptions, even among them. This woman at the machine, for example, was out of the ordinary. Unable to behave like her compatriots, she was ignored by them. She was the only one who had to work at this heavy machine. As I stood near her, she told me a bit about herself.

She had lived in Munich with her husband and their five children. At the outbreak of the war, her husband was mobilized into the army. He was killed a few months later. By working in a factory, she earned a bit to supplement her small government pension to keep her family together. Despite the added income, they suffered from hunger and cold. One day, one of her little boys fell ill. She stayed at home with him. The same day, he died in her arms. In the evening, gendarmes came to her home. Because she missed work, she was sent to the concentration camp for "sabotage." Her four children were left with nobody to take care of them.

I laughed. I asked her if she knew what was happening to the Jews? She did not know. She told me that in Germany it was well known how Hitler was improving the lot of the Jews by organizing them and employing them in the concentration camps.

What a beautiful fairy tale for good children! The German people saw Hitler as God, his word sacred. That is why, amazingly, those that lived several hundred metres away from the camps did not know what was really going on there. All the mass slaughter and massacres were conducted under the cover of concentration work camps. Who could possibly guess the secret hidden behind the innocent-looking little houses with their huge protruding chimneys? How often would people in the free world pass by and think that these people behind the wires were very industrious – *their factories work nonstop!*

Yes, the "factories" worked day and night. We were the fuel for them. But wet wood does not burn well. There were still too many juices inside us. When the machines dry us out completely we shall be good fuel. In our stead, others will come.

I returned to my work station. But there was still no work. The distance between our table and the machines was now conquered, and it occurred to me that the distance was laughably short. The taste of adventure spurred me on. I took a box filled with debris and decided to take it to the very end of our department where the garbage cart stood. It wasn't necessary, but I wanted to have a better look at "my" department.

I walked holding the box in front of me. I looked around curiously. On my left were row upon row of *Presse*, on the right, tables. Half-way through this big hall were the *Presse* used to manufacture *Einsatzstücke*. The last half had *Presse* for the manufacture of *Körper*.[63]

The work with the *Körper* demanded even more effort, attention, and strength than did the *Einsatzstücke*. Only men operated these *Presse*. Stripped to the waist, glistening with dripping sweat, they tensely watched the machines' movement. By listening attentively, they could discern a foreign sound or a change in the machine's rhythm. They waited, ready to stop the machines' operations with their muscles and nerves.

Over time, the machine, stubborn at the beginning, becomes subject to the will of its operator. He sets it in motion. It responds to his slightest gesture and becomes his faithful "friend." But the process is invariably the same. Slowly, unobtrusively, stealthily, the gears are oiled with blood and sweat. The better and stronger the machine works, the worse and weaker its "master."

Who will replace his blood and sweat? What will compensate for his spent energy? A quarter of a loaf of bread? Or maybe a litre of dirty, cold slop?

A machine without oil will seize up. And a human being? Can he continue working, oiled by beatings and by the spectre of death looming before his eyes? He knows that stopping work means death. And not stopping...? Toil until the end, and then, death? But maybe, just maybe, something will intervene in the meantime. What? He doesn't know, it is not important, but maybe...?

The hands grab the machine with more strength, the ear listens attentively to its droning. It is no longer a machine, producing murderous weapons. It is no longer a factory, crawling with SS men, *Kapos*, and a mob of spies lurking to seize upon a moment of inattention or forgetfulness. This is unearthly hope. This is dreamed-of and yearned-for freedom. It is freedom, home, wife, children.

I walk with my box of rubbish and look at these people, bent in hard labour, their bodies covered with sweat, their skin covering bodies so thin that you could see their ribs and bones through it.

Every one of them was a world unto himself, closed, and undefeated. What do they think about? Do they think at all? Mostly, you cannot see their faces bent over the machines. But you can see some of them.

---

63 Literally, "body" or "bulk." *Körper* were the exterior parts of whatever it was that the factory produced. They were in the shape of round cones, wide at the bottom and narrowing to a sharp tip on top.

A man stands not far from the garbage cart, which was my goal. His clean blue shirt shines from afar. On his arm is a yellow band – *Kapo*. The tips of his shining patent leather shoes peek from under his pants, which are ironed with a sharp crease. He twirls a thin bamboo cane while he flirts through the window in the glass wall with a girl working on the *Laufband*.

Taking advantage of the *Kapo*'s diversion, one of the machine operators painfully straightens his neck. One makes the most of every second of slackness. He stretches once, and again. Ah, what a pleasure! It is written all over the operator's face and the faces of those who follow his example. Now I know what they thought about. In their hearts, they bless the girl who caught the *Kapo*'s attention and pray that she might occupy him as long as possible. I smile involuntarily with pleasure. I join them in their moment of respite and in their feelings of pleasure at having duped the authorities, even for a minute.

But danger approaches. The sound of footsteps from the opposite side announces the green uniform of the *Blockführer*.[64] My legs turn to jelly. *My God! What would happen if he stops me and asks questions? I am all alone among the men, far away from my table and my companions.*

Suddenly, everything and everyone around me goes back to work. The machines hum, the *Presse* drone with their particular, monotonous thuds, testifying that the regular, incessant work has resumed. The naked upper bodies of the workers, bent over their colossal machines, look from afar like a brown, moving mass from which it is impossible to identify individuals.

Only the *Kapo*, blue shirt glaring against the drab background, seems to be unaware of the approaching danger. Of course, absolutely nobody has any intention to warn him. Rather, they are inwardly gloating in anticipation of the upcoming row.

This *Kapo* unwittingly becomes my saviour. The *Blockführer*, attracted by the blue shirt, walks quickly toward it, not looking anywhere else. Taking advantage, I quickly emptied the contents of my box and, seemingly matter-of-factly, returned to my place, my wobbly legs dancing a rumba while my heart did the fox-trot. Seated again, I couldn't stop the nervous trembling of my hands and knees.

Everybody at the table was burning with curiosity and eager to hear my report. My cheeks burning, I told them about the scene I had just witnessed. Just finishing, I heard the warning, *Zeks! Zeks!,* that was commonly used

---

64 The *Block* manager.

to signal danger, the approach of either the "Greens"[65] or the "Yellows."[66] Our hands again worked quickly, mechanically, as if the work had never been interrupted at all.

A few minutes later, without lifting our eyes from our work, we heard a lively conversation between two men walking by us. One voice was loud, commanding, the other quiet and submissive. When the voices and steps passed by us, we all lifted our heads as if on command, and confirmed that the two were the *Blockführer* and the *Kapo*, whom the *Blockführer* must have caught red-handed.

There was unusual excitement in the hall. Taking advantage of the momentary absence of authorities, everybody was discussing the episode. I sat very quietly, proud that I was the first to "travel" at our table.

Encouraged by my example, slowly the girls, one after the other, began to "travel." The first was Sala. She took a box, held it with both hands in front of her, and stepped forward smartly, without once glancing back or to the side.

Her striped dress slowly disappears between the machines. Long minutes go by. We do not see Sala returning. In the meantime, the work begins piling up on the table. I begin to work at both Sala's machine and my own. It comes easily to me; after one became used to the work, it was child's play. I felt very lucky, having been assigned to this table where I didn't have to work as hard as the others.[67]

Another few minutes passed. I started to worry. Who knew what might have happened to her on the way? Maybe somebody had stopped her. Maybe something else had happened. Who knows?

I reproached myself. I had set a bad example that could cause unfortunate, even dangerous consequences. Who knew what might have happened? Thank God! Here she is coming back!

Sala looks very funny, shod in two left shoes, her long legs showing under her too-short striped dress. Still, both of her shoes are made of leather. She walks, holding the box under her arm. When she comes near, I see with astonishment that she is carrying *two* boxes. We exchange knowing glances among ourselves. We are dying of curiosity. What could it mean?

---

65 SS, from their green uniforms.

66 *Kapos*, from their yellow armbands.

67 In particular, I thought of the others, the women working on the *Presse*, or Shoshana (my future husband's sister) working in the *Spritzraum*, who could not help but inhale the pressurized paint.

As she draws nearer to our table, Sala, sure now that no danger threatens her, seeing our curiosity, teases us by walking even slower, a triumphant smile on her face. She is driving us mad! Finally, she deigns to sit down and puts the boxes, one on top of the other, on her knee.

Full of curiosity, unable to hold it in any longer, we shower her with questions. And she? Nothing. Unmoved, a smile on her face, she lets us yell.

When we quieted down a little, she started telling her story. She went, as I had, to the garbage cart. Because no one in authority was around, the men laughed and flirted with her. Sala stopped near the cart and began to talk to a man working nearby. The conversation started with questions. Where was she from? Did she meet, maybe, someone from such and such a town, did she know so and so?

Sala also asked them questions. She learned that a man from Miedzyrzecze, her hometown in Poland, worked in the next department, washing mixed metals in acid. She didn't go there to see him because she was afraid. Toward the end of their conversation, the man gave her a box. He did not place it in her hands, because someone could have noticed. He went to the garbage cart and threw the box into it. Sala took it out, hiding it under the box she had brought, and returned to us.

After saying all of this, she uncovered the box. Only her two closest neighbours, Roza and I, saw the treasure. We looked and cried with wonder. In the bottom box lay two potatoes! Two real, raw potatoes. Quickly, she covered the box. It had to be kept a secret. Sala had confidence in us because, sitting next to each other, we had become acquainted, but she wasn't sure of the others.

Two potatoes. What riches! I couldn't get the potatoes out of my head. Thinking about them, I swallowed hard.

Give me your pocketknife.

Sala's voice woke me from my daydream. My pocketknife, with its broken tip was the envy of the whole table. In the whole camp, there were only a few who could boast of possessing a knife. Mostly, they were those who worked in the *Kanada Kommando* or, of course, those who could buy one. A pocketknife cost a half ration of bread. The *Blockhovas* and *Shtubhovas*, who helped themselves to our rations of bread, could afford knives. I had found my knife while working in the *Rollwagen*[68] in the filth. It was my greatest treasure, and I took the utmost care of it, always keeping it in my shoe. I worked hard to take it out of my shoe.

*O.K. Now look out that nobody is coming,* Sala ordered.

---

68 Latrine wagon.

I kept a nervous lookout. One look to the right, one to the left, and from time to time (I couldn't help it) I sneaked a look at what Sala was doing.

I could see that she was cutting a potato into thin slices. Then she took a bit of salt from Roza and salted them. I lifted my head and looked. And I thought, *Lucky Roza!* She had arrived in the camp only a short time earlier and already she had a friend, a *Shtubhova* who gave her a bit more soup and from whom she also got the salt. I wet my lips with my tongue. I jammed my elbow into Sala's side – careful, the foreman is coming!

Quickly, keeping everything on her knees, Sala bent over the table and started working. I was so scared. The foreman had chosen this exact time to stand near our table and look at our work. My hands were shaking. Finally, he moved on.

We breathed a sigh of relief. Now came the main event. Now they will eat. *Will she give me some or not,* I wonder, *yes or no?* I worked eagerly, so as not to look at her, as if I didn't care. I didn't want to betray my want. Suddenly, I felt an elbow in my side and a whisper, *Here, hold it.*

*What is going on?* I try to assume an indifferent tone.

*Here, have a potato!* Sala hands me two slices of potato under the table.

*No, I don't want any. You have very little for yourself.* But quickly I extend my hand under the table and take it. *Who knows, she may change her mind.*

But she didn't. I took little pieces into my mouth, revelling in every bite. Delicious. All three of us were silently eating, totally absorbed, not wanting to miss any of the sensation. I ate one slice and put the second inside the cuff of my sleeve. This would be for Estusia.

But the second slice of potato wouldn't leave me in peace. The first just tickled my hunger, which had been dormant for a while and now was bothering me twice as much. *To eat or not to eat, to eat or not to eat.*

I work with redoubled energy, trying to forget about it. But this little slice grows to huge proportions in my imagination. *Maybe I can bite just a tiny little bit.* I look around carefully to make sure nobody is watching, and unfold the cuff. But, at the very last minute, when my trembling fingers are about to snatch this by now blackened miserable slice, I refold my cuff. *No. No way. I already had a piece and she had had nothing.*

I kept on working. I could think of nothing else but the whistle that announced lunch break. I had heard nothing. I was sure that lunch hour must have long past. Where could I find out what time it was?

I had a bright idea. There was a big clock on the wall not far from the entrance to the toilets. To get permission to go to the toilet, to get up from the table at all, I needed to have a number from the *Kapo.* Our *Kapo* was Alma, whose face and barrel-like body gave her the appearance of a bulldog.

As it happened, Alma was busy flirting with her lover, Hans, a German gypsy. Everything has its good and bad sides, and Alma's love affair with

Hans played into our hands on several occasions. Alma often made inspections of our belongings on her own authority. Our carefully saved remains of the previous night's rations of bread would thus "come into her possession." It was Hans who on occasion succeeded in putting her in a better mood and who made Alma return the bread to us. With Hans at her side, Alma was capable of great generosity to impress her lover.

I got up, quickly, fixed the cuff of my sleeve once again, and went over to Alma. To give myself more credibility, I held my stomach with one hand and, crying in pain, exclaimed, *Kapo, may I be excused?*

Alma, besotted with Hans's presence, gave me a number. I bowed in gratitude and, from the excitement, forgot to hold my stomach. I went out from our department to the corridor, running my finger along the net separating the corridor from the *Kontrolle.*[69]

In the *Kontrolle,* I saw long tables with many bent-over shapes, looking like long necklaces strung with unpolished beads. In between the tables glimmered the gray overalls of the foreman, Rypping, and the black apron of the forewoman, Mimi. Mimi and Rypping were German civilians who supervised the prisoners and their work. Every department had its own civilian foreman and forewoman. There were all kinds, some better, some worse.

But, at this point, the whole world seemed to me to be good. I walked, almost dancing. A great happiness spread through my heart. *I have a slice of potato for Estusia, I tricked Alma, and now I am going to find out what time it is.*

It seemed to me that everything and everyone around me reflected my happiness. All the Jews were smiling, everybody smiled at me, and I smiled at everybody. At this moment, each and every one of them was so dear to me, so close. I just felt like embracing and hugging the whole world.

On that day, it looked as if everything was going my way. Nearing the toilet, even the clock seemed to laugh at me with its round, puffed-out dial. Its hands winked at me, showing two minutes to noon. *Only two more minutes! It's not worthwhile going back. For two minutes, I might as well wait here.*

There were two entrances leading to the bathroom, with signs on each of them: on the left side for Jews, on the right side for Germans. At the far end of the bathroom were doors to the toilets. On each side, there were eight toilets. In front of the Jewish toilets, there was a permanent queue. There were five hundred of us and fifty Germans. Heaven forbid that one of us would dare enter the German toilet! It never happened.

---

69  Quality Control, where the output was checked.

The toilet area was a main source of news and information. It replaced radios and newspapers. It was where all were told and passed on all of the overheard conversations between the foremen, everything that was happening in the different departments in the factory, all the political news.

Some of it was true, some of it was not. Everyone returning to her post repeated the news she acquired. Thus, in a flash, news would spread all over the factory. The toilet area also served as a "post office" and for arranging meetings. When we met girls from other departments, we asked and were asked to relay messages.

Because of the chronic terrible overcrowding at the Jewish toilets, *Oberkapo* Maria, with the help of a few Germans, would chase us out, striking at us, pouring water on us, swearing at us. We knew their curses by heart – *Mist speiende Jude! Ihr faul, dreckig!*[70]

We used to shrink, to try to take as little space as possible, to make ourselves as invisible as possible. The last ones in got the worst of it. They had to return to work, wet, beaten up, without having been able to use the facilities. The lucky ones stayed on. Sometimes their German tormentors would drag out wet, flogged girls, and quarrels would break out among the Germans. The good Germans invariably walked away with the epithet "Jew-friend" flung at their backs.

On the right-hand side, the German side, things were quite different. A lookout stood in front of the entrance. Through the entrance you could see inside the bathroom. There, lost in the permanent semi-darkness, you could see the outline of romantically engaged pairs, illuminated from time to time by lit cigarettes. A cigarette bribe silenced any jealous witness.

I entered the bathroom. It had no tub. Instead, there were showers all along the walls, and in the middle. It had a tiled floor. I stood in the toilet queue, shaking with impatience. *If only* Oberkapo *Maria doesn't come before the lunch gong. I have no desire to return to work.* But the silence outside promised peace. The danger was far away, lurking in some other corner of the factory. Gradually, the hubbub in the toilets increased. At this point, I saw Ròzyczka[71] leaving. She worked with Estusia in the *Pulverraum.*[72]

---

70 "Shit-spewing Jew! You [are] lazy, dirty!"

71 Rose Meth.

72 Gunpowder room (literally, "powder room"). The *Pulverraum* was the only place in the factory that handled gunpowder. The *Pulverraum* was a department located in a small room on the north outside wall of the building. They had a door to the outside, which was open during nice weather, letting fresh air through. The upper part of the door was made of glass, which permitted light in when the door was closed in inclement weather.

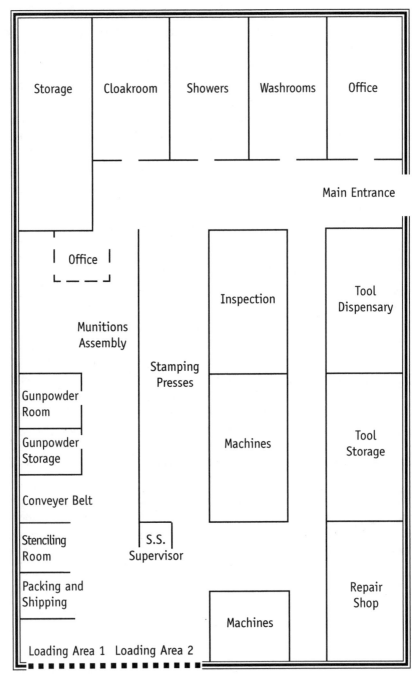

Weichsel Union Munitions Factory floor plan, Auschwitz, 1944,
as remembered by Anna Heilman (not to scale)

*Hi. How are you?* Ròzyczka asks.

*Fine,* I answer. *Tell Estusia that I am here.*

*O.K.*

Ròzyczka disappeared behind the door to the corridor. Now I was calm. I looked at the girls standing near me and a bit farther away. There were all kinds of types. Some were standing in black, oily, rubber aprons, covered with metal filings. Their job was to oil the machines. All day long, they stood on their feet, their hands fumbling around in the dirty oil. The machines squirted oil in all directions. Any uncovered part of their body immediately was covered with blisters and pimples – and their faces, hands, and arms up past the elbows were covered with metal filings.

They could hardly stand on their feet from the enormous heat. The oily clothes stuck to their bodies, the grease seeped through their aprons, through their shirts, down to their socks and shoes. Near them, I could see others, with attractive, black, shiny, well-ironed aprons worn over neat striped dresses decorated with hand-made white, pink, or blue collars.

Since the material for their collars was cut off their slips, the colour of their collars depended upon the colour of their slips. The thread came from blankets; the needles were borrowed from the girls who worked in the tailor-shop *Kommando*. These outfits looked neat and prim but of course had to fit the work environment. You couldn't wear them at machines that spewed a lot of oil. In our department, too, it was hard keeping the aprons and collars clean. Our aprons and collars always had a layer of yellow dust on them.

The neatest girls were those working on the *Montage* and at the *Laufband*. Scrupulous cleanliness was necessary to ensure that the manufactured product was made to precision tolerances. This created ideal hygienic conditions. These girls differed from us in their neatness and appearance and thus became the stars of the factory.

I stood near the entrance, but there was still no sign of Estusia. I let those behind me go first. They were impressed with my politeness.

In the few minutes available to them in the toilets, everybody wanted to exchange news to share with their comrades. I could hear the noise of all the languages of Europe being mixed together. Fragments of conversations flew in and out of my ears. I was not listening, absorbed with my own secret, but unwillingly some words penetrated my consciousness.

*Anna-Lisa has been running around like a mad dog since this morning!,* I hear. Unteroffizier[73] *did not come and she was very upset. I am telling*

---

73  A corporal, or petty officer.

*you, I can hardly stand it! All day long she hovers over us like an executioner over a head. Of course, there is no question of getting a number.*[74]

*Never mind,* answers her friend. *Our foreman is also running around all day long and whispering with the foreman from* Kontrolle. *You know, that madman. And Ala was in the office today and says that something doesn't add up, she saw the* Meister *so absorbed with his newspaper that he didn't even notice her coming in. I have to run. Don't tell anybody.*

Now I understand why Estusia isn't here yet. Anna-Lisa is the civilian supervisor for Estusia's department, and she's the reason why Estusia cannot get out. The prolonged wail of the factory siren momentarily blows away my worry.

Lunch! The toilet area empties in a second. I run quickly to my table for my spoon. In the meantime, in the corridor,[75] everyone runs to line up.

I am sure we won't get any lunch today. We will be at the very end. I am the last one at the table. I grab my spoon and wait for Estusia near the storeroom. The girls from the *Montage* and *Laufband* flash past my eyes. A German pushes me and orders me to line up.

*Estusia, where are you? Maybe she has already gone by and I missed her? Maybe she went by a long time ago and is now standing at the very front of the line? No, it can't be.* I distance myself from the German and slowly walk backward.

Then I hear, *Hanka! Finally! I didn't know what to think! Why are you always the last one? But come now, quickly. Let's line up.* Careful, Estusia pulls me by my apron. Ròzyczka, Estusia, and I, that makes three of us. Two more girls and we will have a row of five; otherwise, we will be kicked out.

*Hey!* I call two girls from the rear.

*Shut your mouth, you louse!* Maria started her count of the rows. *Can't you stand quietly?*

Estusia is the first to talk. *Yeah, all I need is to have you make it worse. Haven't I already had a bad enough day?*

I answer angrily, *Why couldn't you hurry up a bit? If it wasn't for you, I would be in the first row.*

*You have no idea what was going on today,* Estusia answers, *Quiet! Not now, we are moving!*

---

74  I think you needed a number to get into the washroom, even at noon. Otherwise, it would have been mobbed.

75  The corridor outside the washroom was also the corridor leading to the lunch area.

Indeed, though we couldn't see any movement ahead of us, the distinctive clatter of clogs against the cement floor indicated that the first rows had started to move. Then the rows ahead of us started moving, and then we were moving too. In the silence, only the *knack, knack* of the clogs could be heard. I furtively gave Estusia the potato slice that I had kept for her.

We went out into the factory courtyard. The cold immediately stabbed us. The sharp drizzle, driven by gusts of wind, cuts across our faces and right through us. I couldn't control my shivering.

We were standing in pairs. By now, standing close for warmth, I looked back and saw that there were still enough people behind us.[76] We moved forward slowly. As we got closer to the distribution point we heard screams and beatings.

*Who is at the kettle?*[77]

*Alma,* comes the response.

On both sides of the rows, individuals moved furtively. Those from behind were trying to get there first.

*Hallo, where do you think you are going?*

*Don't let them in!*

The Germans came up the rows, hitting on the left and on the right.

*Everybody on their knees!* screamed Maria.

We knelt on the soggy ground and waited. Slowly, we moved forward on our knees. Finally, Alma poured some food in my bowl. I could feel its warmth through the thin tin. I warmed my hands and greedily started to drink, but, at the very first gulp, my lips curled with distaste. *Nettles are nettles, whether they are raw or boiled. But there is no choice, at least it is warm.*

On the other side of the wires, opposite the *Pulverraum* and across the road, were carpentry shops on which were written "O.B.W." These workshops were surrounded by high wires, just as the factory was. I looked with great interest at the male prisoners who were working there. They were also on their lunch break. We exchanged glances. They were about fifteen metres away. So near, and so far. We cannot speak to them, and so many questions are pushing against our closed lips.

Instead, we have a silent conversation. We understand each other. We recognize each other by our numbers. The numbers with yellow stars are

---

76 That is, enough people behind us to ensure that we would still get some food.

77 The kettle-drum from which the food was served.

the Jews. Those with red, black, and green triangles are Germans, Poles, Russians, and others.

*Where are they from? Why are they here? How do they live?* The dull, mournful sound of the siren calls us back to work, interrupting my musing. We hasten back and entering, breathe deeply, delightfully, the stinking, dusty, but warm air.

The afternoon passes quickly. Just about five in the afternoon, a wonderful smell of broth fills the air. This is the special supplement for people working at the heavy machines. The smell tickles our nostrils and twists our insides. We, the ordinary mortals, have to satisfy ourselves just with the smell. To think that behind our wires, so close as to almost touch them, live people who have no idea what the remnants of their meals, left so carelessly on their plates, would mean to us. *Are they aware of our existence? Do they realize what hell we live in? Do they ever ask themselves where the hundreds of thousands of people who pass their towns and hamlets in closed cattle cars or in trucks go?*

Trembling with apprehension, we dared to walk from department to department, furtively exchanging a few words with the men, looking around for the yellow armband of a *Kapo* or the green of a German uniform. How much hope and confidence these little outings gave us!

On the whole, the men used to help us a lot. Now and then, while passing by, they would furtively throw us a warm word of greeting, encouragement, and hope that raised our morale. The men gave us courage with a word in our most difficult moments, in times of depression and breakdown. Sometimes, when something was found on one of us, they tried to protect us from being beaten and tried to prevent our being sent to the *Bunker*, the dreaded prison-within-the-prison.

Many helped by giving us food parcels. Wherever possible, they would throw us a piece of bread, a potato, and even occasionally a cigarette, which was worth its weight in gold. They were always full of optimism. Most of the time at the women's camp, the atmosphere was heavy and relations between women were hostile, but at the men's camp there appeared to be more solidarity.

While sitting at the table, we often saw people running, carrying a victim of an accident at work. It might be a man crushed by a heavy press. It might be a man with his arm dangling, or a man who had lost his fingers in the machine's gears. They were given first aid in the *Ambulanz*, then sent away to the camp. Those unable to work were finished off. In their place came new victims, to make weapons against themselves and to nourish the parasites on their own bodies.

Exhausted and spent, we would return to the camp at the end of a twelve-hour-long workday. I eagerly and impatiently awaited that moment, a time when we could meet with our friends and chat, to tell them the day's events, to listen to them, and then to talk about all kinds of subjects. We used to sit in the field behind the *Blocks*, under the carts. During the day, women worked hard pushing these carts after filling them with heavy rocks. Our talks lasted late into the night.

While silence reigned in the camp, leaning close to each other, we whispered for a long time, the moon and the stars our witnesses. Our group was enlarged by a few Russian and Yugoslav girls. They had contact with partisans in the free world, and we thus gained some knowledge about the political situation, about the partisans' activities, about a tunnel dug in the men's camp through which small groups of men escaped daily.

Indeed, returning from work, we often heard the wail of a siren announcing an escape. We would be ecstatic. It is true that, following each escape, as punishment, the men had to stand on *Appel* for long hours without food, and many innocents screamed from the pain of the riding crops. Still, nobody complained; it was worth it. It was worth the suffering. It paid for the lives of heroes.

There was only one escape. It ended in tragedy. A young girl, Mala Zimetbaum, came to the camp on one of the first transports from Belgium. Right away she was made a *Läuferin*,[78] a privileged and responsible position. Through her demeanour, she gained the sympathy and confidence of the SS men and SS women administrators with whom she worked. She knew how to take advantage of it. Her position allowed her to help those around her enormously, especially her Belgian friends. Thanks to her, many were saved from selections. Mala gave many a better chance of surviving and an easier life in the camp by arranging their placement in "good" *Kommandos*.

While in camp, Mala met a Polish man. One day, she escaped with him. Mala was well known in the camp and universally liked, so everybody was euphoric.

They looked for her everywhere, but didn't find her. After a few days, the incident paled and was almost forgotten, only to erupt again with even greater force three weeks later. Like a bolt of lightning from a clear sky, the news exploded that Mala and her friend had been caught. Some men said that they had seen Mala being marched into the *Bunker*, others said that it was not Mala. Nobody knew for sure.

While returning from work one evening, we passed four girls carrying a stretcher. On the stretcher was a bloodied figure, her face turned away so it couldn't be seen. But some of the girls recognized her anyway. Mala.

---

78  A runner or messenger.

A terrible feeling overcame me. There was a great commotion in the camp. Small groups of girls stood around, talking. All had tears in their eyes. *What happened?* we asked, *What happened?* But nobody could answer. We heard only one word. *Mala. Mala.* We ran over to our own friends and learned everything.

Early in the morning, between the old and new camps[79] a few men, under the watchful eye of the *Blockführer*, began pounding and hammering. They erected a pole with ropes. Nobody knew what it was. We were ordered there in the evening after *Appel*. Mala was brought out.

Now we understood what was going to happen. There was total silence, interrupted only by the lecturing *Lagerkommandant*. Mala stood on one side and rummaged for something in her *Beutel*.[80] Suddenly, the *Blockführer* jumped on Mala. The silence was broken by the loud sound of a slap. There was blood on Mala's wrist.

While the *Lagerkommandant* was talking, this brave girl had decided to deny them the show and to thwart their plans for her execution. She cut her wrist with a dull razor blade. The *Blockführer* had noticed and tried to stop her, but he was too late. She had had enough presence of mind to slap him off and push him away. She was taken to the *Revier*, but died on the way. By the time that we arrived, it was all over.

I felt terrible. Just now, when we needed people like her, she was taken from us. Brave, courageous heroine. *They did not succeed in doing what they intended with you.* One more heroic deed in Jewish history.

We did not talk that evening, although there were so many important things to talk about. We sat until late, each deeply immersed in her own thoughts. We parted without speaking, not willing to break the solemn silence. We could not sleep that night. I did not know Mala personally, yet I felt that she was standing near me, her pale face smiling, her bloody hand held high, saying to me, *I started; you finish.* And I did not feel so bad anymore. I gritted my teeth and told myself, *We go on.*

And life went on. I sat at my table in the factory, but could hardly stop my eyes from closing and my head from dropping to the table. No wonder. We were going to sleep at 2 a.m. and getting up at 4 a.m. I sleepwalked to work.

But it didn't matter. My fantasies were becoming reality. The Russians were nearing Warsaw.

---

79  Camps A and B in Birkenau.

80  A cloth sack with a drawstring in which each of us used to keep all our earthly possessions.

# The October 1944 Uprising[1]

By now, it must have been June or July 1944. We had been in Birkenau for a year. We were old-timers. The work at Union provided us a measure of security and comfort. We were working indoors, and, through the generous offices of the civilian German foreman, our food improved considerably. We spent most of the day away from the camp, away from its daily brutalities, away from the crematoria now fuelled non-stop by the transports from Hungary.

We developed close friendships with a group of girls in the camp, with whom we met in the evenings. We lived for those evenings. They helped us to escape the reality and gave us the moral courage to survive with dignity. Slowly, very much as in the Warsaw ghetto, the warmth and closeness of our company overtook the reality of our circumstances. We sang songs and told stories; we lived in our dreams.

Though this group consisted only of Jewish girls, there was one girl who wore a red triangle on her number, identifying her as a Pole. She was Jewish, but had succeeded in maintaining her false identity as a non-Jew. This girl[2] was either directly involved with the Polish Underground or was close enough to them to have gained their confidence. She used to supply us with current political news.

There was great excitement in our group when one night in August 1944 she shared with us the news that the Red Army was closing in on Warsaw and would soon overrun it.

We knew that if they continued at this speed they could reach us in two or three weeks. We were quite resigned to the prospect that before the Russians came, the Germans would finish us off.

---

1 This section consists of memoirs written in 1993 in Ottawa, Canada.

2 How I wish I could remember her name!

She told us that the Polish Home Army was organizing a revolt in Warsaw, that they were in contact with the Polish Underground in Auschwitz,[3] that they had spread the word that we should get organized on the inside. On a given password, they were supposed to attack the camp from the outside, and we were to be ready to help them from the inside.

*What could we do to help?* We were ecstatic, in a state of euphoria. Estusia and I talked about the revolt in the Warsaw ghetto. We told them, *If it could be done there, it can be done here.*

Work began to implement the plan. Slowly, carefully, we spread the word. There were many volunteers, non-Jews as well as Jews. We were in contact with the men. They were getting ready too, even more than we. They seemed to have more resources.

We started amassing matches, gasoline, and all kinds of heavy objects at agreed-upon spots. In the following days, we secured the keys to the farm tool shed. I understood that, at the password, we were supposed to use the keys to the tool shed so that we could take the rakes, hoes, and other implements stored inside to use as weapons.

In each *Block*, there was a group of four or at most six girls involved in the plan. Each group had a leader who was responsible for collecting these objects and directing the work. Only the group leaders knew each other; the members of the groups had no idea who the other group members were. The leader in each *Block* had contact with "headquarters." The work continued. The conspiracy was tight.

One day in the Union factory, I approached a Yugoslav man who worked in the *Schlosserei*.[4] I had never talked to him before but used to pass him on my way to the toilet. He always smiled at me.

I threw caution to the wind and asked him if he could provide me with a pair of insulated wire-cutting sheers. We could use them to cut through the electrified wires around the camp. He looked at me. He didn't say a word. I spent a few anxious days worrying about the consequences of my folly.

Lo and behold! One day, he came over and put a box in front of me. The girls at the table teased me about my "lover." I put the box quickly under my chair, but I managed to peek into it. There was a whole loaf of bread inside! I was delighted, but a bit disappointed. I was glad that I could trust him and overjoyed at this unexpected bounty, the first and

---

3  My understanding was that the Polish Underground excluded Jews. We ourselves were not part of it, nor were we aware of its existence in Auschwitz until this time.

4  Locksmith's workshop.

only I ever received from him. Luckily, there was no inspection that day, and I brought my bread safely into the camp in my *Beutel*.

These inspections occurred about once a month as we were lined up outside of the factory in rows of five after work on our way back to camp. They were always unexpected. The *Kapos* would yell, *Kontrol!* – and would run between the rows searching all of us for all kinds of contraband. After each inspection, the ground was strewn with *Beutels*. They were all confiscated. After the search, they kept anything that was worth keeping. Designated girls chosen at random had to pick up what was left over and throw it into the garbage. Each of us manufactured a new *Beutel* the next day.

Since we worked with the men in the factory, it was well known that they would slip us food parcels and little trinkets. Also, we were not supposed to have any personal possessions, yet everybody had them, so all of it – be it toothbrushes, combs, pieces of string, pieces of material, you name it – was confiscated. Little things were overlooked. More serious matters, like possession of a whole loaf of bread, were punished by kicking, yelling, beating, and forcing the girls to name their benefactors. The standard response was, *I found it.*

Once back in camp on our bed, I showed Estusia what I had gotten. Hiding our treasure from spying eyes with our bodies, we inspected it. To our amazement, the bread was hollowed out. Inside we saw a pair of beautiful wire-cutting sheers with red insulated handles. We couldn't believe it. So the folly had paid off. We hid the wire-cutters in our mattress, hoping and praying that nobody would find them.

We shared our bed with Ròzyczka and three other girls. The bed on our left was occupied by Sala, my potato benefactor, Ala Gertner, and a newcomer, Klara, a girl from Russia. We befriended Klara, who was the supervisor on the night shift at Union, and on whom Estusia and I practised our Russian, as Russian was actually our mother tongue.[5] Though we were friendly with Klara, we never included her in our nightly meetings, repulsing her attempts to get too chummy with us.[6]

That evening, we shared the secret of our new acquisition with our friends. We felt it was a prudent thing to do. If something happened in the camp while we were at work, they would have access to it.

---

5 My mother was born and educated in "Russia" while Poland was under Russian control. She never learned Polish.

6 For some reason, Klara was not trusted. Her transport story didn't ring true, and she appeared to have come from nowhere.

One evening, Ala told us that she had a friend named Roza Robota, who worked at the *Bekleidungskammer*.[7] Roza had a lover[8] in the *Sonderkommando*. This lover had told her that he felt sure the time was drawing near when the *Sonderkommando* were to be murdered.

It was common knowledge that, after a few months of service, the *Sonderkommando* were killed and new "workers" were brought in to replace them. He told Roza that they had heard about the Russian Army coming closer, that the Polish Home Army was preparing an uprising and an onslaught on Auschwitz. The *Sonderkommando* were arming themselves and waiting for the password.

That night, I had an idea. We didn't have weapons. What we were collecting was better than nothing, but not much. But then we could use gunpowder.... I talked to Estusia about trying to steal gunpowder from the factory and passing it to Roza. Estusia was aghast. She wouldn't hear of it. It was impossible, ridiculous, forget it. I wouldn't let her be. Finally, with trepidation, she gave in.

We thus began to smuggle gunpowder. I routinely would get up from my table, turn left at the corridor, turn right under the nose of the civilian foreman in his glass cage, walk around it, turn left again past the storage area, and stop in front of the *Pulverraum* door.

The four girls working in the *Pulverraum* could see the men passing in their *Kommandos* and sometimes would exchange greetings. This is how Estusia met Tadek, a Polish *Kapo*. The girls' supervisor was a Jewish girl, Regina Safirztajn. The girls had small presses mounted on the table top. They sat in a row, each facing her own machine.

Their job was to press small quantities of gunpowder into little holes of the *Einsatzstücke* that the big presses manufactured, and which my department checked for precision. The gunpowder was slate gray, almost black, having the consistency of coarse salt.

Estusia's seat was the first leading to the inside door of the factory. I used to stand in front of this door, where Estusia would give me a small metal box.

These boxes were used for all sorts of garbage, which was emptied into large garbage bins that stood in the corners of each department and

---

7 The clothing *Kommando*.

8 "Having a lover" meant to have a male protector. I don't know if they had sexual relationships. Perhaps some did. Usually, they were men who had passes to enter the women's camp – handymen, electricians, plumbers, etc. The *Sonderkommando* were men who had access to riches, for obvious reasons. It was easy for them to bribe the authorities and come in.

sometimes along the walls. Different prisoners at different times swept the floors and emptied the dust and sweepings into these bins.

Once a day, I would walk in with an empty box, give it to Estusia, and get a box full of debris from her to be emptied into the garbage bin. Estusia would put small quantities of gunpowder wrapped in pieces of knotted cloth hidden among the garbage.

We refined the routine. On my return trip, I carried two boxes from the *Pulverraum*, one on top of the other. I would deposit one of the boxes in the garbage bin. I would bring the other box back with me, setting it on the floor under my table. There were many boxes like these under the table because the *Einsatzstücke* that we checked were brought to us and taken away in the same kind of box. While under the table, I would stuff the little packages inside my dress. My arrival at the *Pulverraum* would signal Ala to go and meet me at the toilet. There we would divide and hide the gunpowder on our bodies, inside our bras.

Somehow, nobody questioned me. Everybody must have assumed that somebody else gave me this additional responsibility. I became a familiar figure, walking around with boxes and emptying them in the garbage.

It was impossible for Estusia to smuggle out any gunpowder because she and her comrades were body-searched every time they left the *Pulverraum*. On the way back to camp, we would divide the powder among the three of us. We made sure to be in the middle of the column, never at the end, never at the beginning.

When the dreadful word "inspection" would sound, we had enough time to unknot our little bundles, spread the gunpowder beneath us, and use our feet to mix it into dirt on the ground, which was covered with the litter of abandoned *Beutels*. While they were looking for all kinds of contraband, they certainly weren't looking for gunpowder.

Despite the inspections, we succeeded in bringing the gunpowder into the camp. Ala would then give it to Roza, who deposited it at the wires near the crematorium, where her lover would pick it up.[9] Time passed. We were living on adrenaline, suspended between fear and excitement.

---

9 The *Sonderkommando* had access to the women's camp. One of their jobs was to carry away corpses from the camp. I think the reason that Roza didn't give the gunpowder to her "lover" directly was for their own security. We were surrounded by people who constantly watched everything we did. Leaving it by the wires meant that no one could testify that parcels were exchanged between them.

One day in October 1944,[10] there was an awful commotion in Auschwitz. The *Sonderkommando* revolted. They succeeded in blowing up one of the crematoria[11] before the SS killed all of them on the spot.

We were at work in the factory when the revolt occurred. We were dumbfounded. There had been no planned date for the uprising. No password had been given. We had all been waiting to hear from the PPR or PPS. What had happened?

Slowly, bits and pieces of information reached us. It seemed that there had been an informer among the *Sonderkommando* who got wind of the preparations for the uprising and who betrayed them to the SS.

The ensuing investigation revealed the presence of hand-made grenades that were ignited by small wicks. The grenades were made out of shoe polish boxes[12] filled with gunpowder. The gunpowder was identified as coming from the Union factory, and in the Union factory, from the *Pulverraum.*[13]

Questioning and further investigation from October to December 1944 produced nothing.[14] Ròzyczka was interrogated and horribly beaten, but she did not reveal anything. One day, an inspection in the *Pulverraum* revealed a package of goodies – food. The package was a present that Estusia had received from the Polish *Kapo*, Tadek, who had recently befriended her.

---

10  October 7, 1944.

11  There were five crematoria at Auschwitz. The one that was destroyed during the uprising was Crematorium IV.

12  The shoe polish boxes were standard round metal boxes. They came, like everything else, from the transports. The wicks for the grenades were made from braided pieces of cotton.

13  Apparently, each lot of gunpowder had its own characteristic and could be identified and traced back to its origin, although we didn't know it.

14  It might strike many as curious that the Germans bothered investigating rather than simply killing everyone who could conceivably have had anything to do with the gunpowder smuggling and start over again with new "employees." However, while the transports consisted of nameless people and it was standard procedure either to gas them immediately or to gas them after a period of slave labour in the camp when they were no longer useful, an act of sabotage was something else. I imagine (though don't know for sure) that the Nazis knew very well that there was an organized resistance in the camp and maybe they wanted to get to the leaders of the resistance through torturing the girls. Since they were not a part of the organized resistance, they couldn't tell them anything. They did tell them the names of the *Sonderkommando* crew, since they were dead by then and no further harm could be done.

In the meantime, the Union *Kommando* was transferred from Birkenau to Auschwitz itself, a distance of a few kilometres.[15] Our new quarters were luxurious, in two-storey brick buildings. Upstairs were wooden beds with decent mattresses, individual blankets, all spotless. Downstairs were showers with real hot water. It meant decent living conditions, proper hygiene, and a much shorter walk to work. There was even a cinema to which we were ordered to go one night.

The investigation proceeded without much progress. Rumour had it that there was an inspection on the night shift in the Union factory. Klara, our Klara,[16] was found with a parcel of bread. She was beaten, but would not betray her boyfriend. Instead, she told the Germans that, if they let her go, she would tell them who was involved in the gunpowder smuggling. She betrayed Ala sometime between late October and early November 1944.

Ala was taken for questioning. After a terrible beating, she broke down and denounced Roza and Estusia.[17] All three were taken to the *Bunker*, a prison in the men's camp under the control of the Jewish *Kapo,* Jakub. They were tortured mercilessly.

I was beside myself with grief and horror. I was told that a young Belgian Jew who worked at the stamping presses had contact with the Polish Underground. I did not care about the consequences. I approached him at work and begged him to bring me word from Estusia, to tell me what the girls were saying so that I could back their stories. He chased me away angrily and told me never to come near him. He didn't want to be seen with me. I felt completely betrayed and at a total loss.

One day, I was dragged to the office in the Union factory by my *Kapo*, Alma. In the office was *Oberkapo* Maria, two SS officers – one rough, one kind (the "good cop/bad cop" routine) – and the civilian foreman, von Ender. Maria slapped me around but von Ender put a stop to it almost immediately. The "kindly" SS man led me to a chair and gave me a kerchief to wipe my bloody face.

In fatherly tones, he questioned me: *Who stole the gunpowder? Why? Where? What did your sister tell you?* I sat there looking at him dumbly. He continued by saying there was no use denying it further because Estusia had confessed everything.

I looked straight at him and said, *How can Estusia confess to anything? She is innocent and she is not a liar. She would never lie.*

---

15  I don't know why they transferred us.

16  The untrusted Russian girl.

17  I am not sure why she didn't betray me. Maybe she focused on Roza and the *Pulverraum*.

He smiled. They let me go. They released the three girls a few days later. Estusia returned, more dead than alive. She was black and blue from head to toe. The skin on her back was broken in stripes. She couldn't move; she couldn't talk. Marta and I tended to her. She improved slowly. We hoped fervently that it was over.

On December 1, we celebrated my birthday. Marta contributed to the occasion by making a rice pudding, which she put on the window sill to cool.[18] We spread a cloth on our upper bed and celebrated Estusia's return and my birthday. When the time came for the pudding, it was gone. Somebody had stolen it.

Suddenly, all our friends abandoned us, nobody wanted to be seen with us, except Ròzyczka and Marta. We cherished our days together, in our isolation. After a few days, Estusia, Ala, and Ròza were taken away again, accompanied by poor innocent Regina Safirztajn. Regina was not involved in the gunpowder smuggling but was taken because she was the supervisor responsible for the *Pulverraum*.

I went mad. Marta bribed Dora Klein, a Jewish woman prisoner–physician, to get me into the *Revier*. Marta was afraid that I would throw myself on the electrified wires surrounding the camp. Since she worked in the men's camp in the *Packerei*, she became the go-between for Estusia and me.

## Premonition[19]

Here and there the white uniforms of wandering doctors and nurses. But they, too, slowly disappear. Everything is silent. Trees bend sadly towards each other as if sharing secrets, crumpled blades of grass straighten up slowly. Multicoloured flowers flirt with bees, flies, and butterflies. Golden rays dance playfully, awakening everything to life. Birds lift themselves high into the air, singing hymns of thanksgiving in the sky.

---

18  Marta worked in the *Packerei* (camp post office). The non-Jewish inmates were allowed mail and packages. Sometimes, when the packages couldn't be delivered (for whatever reason), the staff got the packages. Marta brought the rice. With rice and hot water, one could make rice pudding, and Marta did. The *Aufseherin* responsible for this small *Kommando* was very protective of her workers and was their great friend. Marta and Aniczka worked there. Marta used to provide Estusia and me with all kinds of "goodies" that she shared. In the blocks were wood stoves that, if you were a friend of the *Blockhova* who happened to be Marta's cousin, you could cook anything, provided you had something to cook.

19  This section consist of diary material originally written in Auschwitz in Polish in November 1944, destroyed in a search, and rewritten from memory in 1945 in the Ardennes,

All together, it creates a wonderful morning ambiance, a smell that no perfume can replicate, the melody unheard and not understood by people.

Who could imagine the scene that took place in this beguiling corner just a few hours ago?

Who could imagine how much blood was spilled here and how many lost their lives?

Maybe the birds are twittering about it? Or maybe the trees are whispering, secretly moving their silvery crowns? Or maybe the grasshoppers are playing it on their fiddles? But who can understand it? Who would be able to uncover nature's secrets, stored for hundreds and thousands of years?

Along a narrow path, a shape trudges through the fields. It is difficult to call this shape, struggling forward on all fours, a human being. Through the bloody mask that once might have been a face, only the brilliant, fuelled-by-fever eyes can be seen. Bloodied strips of his clothing encase him in a hard shell. He moves slowly, laboriously, hardly breathing. Stops. Moves again. Moves, persevering to reach his goal. And his goal is a house whitening the horizon not too far away. Ah! The sight of the house gives him strength. He thinks of the hot bath awaiting him, of the table set with food, of the bed with clean, white sheets.

He thinks of his people, people who should welcome him like their own child. Because he is a hero, returning from a battle for his country and the liberty of his people. Only three more steps to reach his goal. Two more steps. Here he is!

---

Belgium. When I wrote the original text in Auschwitz, I didn't know whether I would live or die. I felt the dilemma that if any of us did make it out, no one would believe us. At the time, Estusia was being interrogated. I didn't know what was happening. I also didn't know what the girls were saying or not saying, and I needed to know in case I was questioned again. I approached a Belgian Jew working in the Union munitions plant for information. I thought he had contacts in the Polish Underground. He didn't want to have anything to do with me and was worried he'd come under suspicion if he spoke with me. I felt betrayed and lost – a pariah.

The story is an expression of my feelings at the time. I also felt strongly alienation and incomprehension when writing the material the following year in Ardennes after my liberation. People did not know how to treat survivors or behave toward them. Instead, they looked at survivors as if we were from another planet.

There was a further sense of isolation because there was no common language between survivors and people who hadn't had the experience. They didn't want to hear about what happened. No one asked, *"Where were you? What happened?"* Even after liberation, I felt like the metaphoric "he" in the story. The ironic thing is that I wrote the story, which turned out to be prescient, in Auschwitz.

He crouches before the closed doors, his heart pounding. Slowly he lifts his hand and knocks. Knocks and listens. Silence. Knocks again. Oh, he can hear steps! His heart pounds even harder, sweat pearls his brow. The door opens slowly.

Suddenly there is a cry, accompanied by a kick, *Away, you lout!*

The door closes. Silence reigns. A silence so deep that it rings in his ears. What happened? He only knows that the door is closed, hostile and unreachable. With his remaining strength he turns around, takes a few steps, and falls on the green grass. He greedily drinks the mist off the grass. In his sick, feverish brain he sees different images, as through a kaleidoscope.

He sees a five-year-old boy, standing at attention in front of his brigade of lead soldiers, facing the portrait of a famous knight and promising himself that when he grows up he will be a brave knight as well.

Now he sees this boy fifteen years later. He is all grown up now, in a real military uniform with beautiful shining gold buttons, a glittering sword at his side. His heart bursts with pride and zeal. He goes to war. He sees the tearstained face of his mother, who for the last time pats his head with a trembling hand. He hears, oh how well he hears his own voice: *Don't cry mommy, I'm coming back, you'll see. I'll come back a hero!*

The image changes again. He sees rows and rows of young soldiers like himself, marching in step, a song on their lips and enthusiasm in their hearts. Row upon row of soldiers like himself, innocent and naive, marching voluntarily into death's arms.

Suddenly there is a tremendous crash and glare. A cloud of dust mixed with stones covers everything. Through the mist there are cries – *Mother! Mother!*

Body parts fly in the air. An order is heard, the decimated rows realign. The same scene repeats itself. His skin grows numb; his hair stands on end.

He was ordered to run, so he runs, he runs forward, not knowing where he is going. Bloodied flakes fly in front of his eyes, his sweat-glued hair falls on his forehead. He has lost his rifle, and his hat as well. He does not want his coat with golden buttons anymore; he does not want to be a hero anymore. He wants to go home, to mommy!

But when he came home – not his own, but still to his countrymen, they told him, *Away, you lout!*

*Mommy, please tell me the truth! Are there no heroes?*

**Estusia's Last Letter**[20]

I remember your last letter as if it were today:

> *I hear the footsteps of the prisoners banging on the ground above my head, the murmur of people returning after a long day of work to their* Block *to rest. Through the bars of my window, the stingy gray ray of light tries to break in, the ray of sunset broken by shadows of many pairs of passing feet.*
>
> *The familiar sounds of the camp – the screams of the* Kapos, *the screams for* czaj,[21] *for soup, for bread, all those hated sounds now seem so precious to me and so soon to be lost. Those outside of my window still have hope, but I have nothing; everything is lost for me. Not for me the glad tidings of forthcoming salvation, not for me the* czaj, *the* Appel, *everything is lost and I so want to live.*

Dear, dear Estusia. I want you near me. I want to be with you. A transport of patients is going to the men's camp today. Jakub told Slawka[22] to bring me. I will see you for sure. My darling, don't give up hope. I believe everything will be all right.

I get up from bed and get dressed with trembling hands. For the first time, an emotion replaces my usual apathy. Today I shall see you. Dr. Tetmaier enters the ward, looking at the list of patients scheduled to go. I stand on the side and wait. My heart pounds. Now.

*And you, what do you have?* I hear a voice like through a fog.

*I ... I ... I ...* I stammer incoherently, feeling myself blush.

*I ... I ... I need X-rays.*

*X-rays? What is wrong with you?*

*I have the flu.*

*Well, I am sorry, we have too many patients today.*

*Dr. Slawka promised, a long time ago, that I would go, but there were always too many patients. And today I got dressed just for the outing. Well, we shall see.* I begin to cruise the ward. *Slawka, where are you?* She is busy.

Finally, she enters the ward. Immediately, the place falls silent. I feel, as always, how my heart begins to throb at the sight of this adored woman.

---

20  This section consists of diary material written in the Ardennes, Belgium, in July 1945. It contains Estusia's last letter to me before her execution. Jakub gave the letter to Marta, who, in turn, gave it to me. I subsequently rewrote the letter from memory.

21  Tea.

22  Dr. Slawka (a pseudonym for Dora Klein). I don't know why she used a pseudonym.

I see her searching for me with her eyes, but my legs are glued to the floor and I cannot move. I stand, leaning against a pillar. Slawka comes toward me. My cramped larynx can't utter a word. I look at her, questioningly. I can hardly hear her voice. It seems to be coming from far away.

*Hanka, you cannot go today. You will go another time. Anyway, don't think that Jakub will be standing around waiting for you. He is too big a celebrity and has a lot on his mind.*

Like a robot, I return to my bed and get undressed, not paying attention to anybody, as if nothing had happened. I feel nothing, no bitterness, no pain. I lie down and trace the knots in the wooden planks of my bed with my fingers. Dusk fights the weakly lit lamps outside. They are distributing supper.

Outside, I see *Kommandos* returning from work. As she does every day, Martuszka[23] comes, her arms full of big and small packages. I look at her with unseeing eyes.

*Hanka, Haneczka, listen to me! Can you hear me? Tell me, how are you? I have good news for you from Estusia!*

*What?* I ask, not caring.

*Listen, the pardon order arrived today from Berlin! Do you hear me?*

*What!* I sat up as if propelled, not believing my ears. *What? When are they going to be let free?*

*We don't know yet – but everything is arranged, Jakub arranged everything. Now, eat!*

*No, I can't but tell me, is it true?*

Could it be? In a few days we could be reunited? Yes, I am sure. Martuszka had to leave me to go to *Appel*. In the meantime, the patients returned from the men's camp.

*Listen,* I ask one, *was Jakub there?*

*Oh, the fat one from the* Bunker, *yeah!*

*Did you notice if he spoke with Slawka?*

*No, I didn't pay attention.*

Out of my mind, I put on my bathrobe (a gift from Marta[24]). I cruise all over the ward, pestering everyone who was at the men's camp. Some hadn't seen or noticed Jakub, others, busy with their own problems, hadn't paid attention, others saw Slawka in conversation with Jakub. Slowly, the visitors leave; the ward empties. It is lights out.

---

23  Marta.

24  Through her work in the *Packerei*, Marta could buy anything.

Leaning on a pillar, I look at the strip of land lit by two lamps on the poles that hold the electrified wires. The utter silence on the ward is interrupted only by the sounds of the sleeping. On my toes, I change position and sit on the floor opposite the wood stove. I look at the square of light on the floor, reflecting the fire through the not-quite-closed doors of the stove. The square quivers and changes its shape, trembling as if possessed with its own life.

I open the stove door wide and look at the coal, burning white, tongues of flames jumping from one piece of coal to another. I look at the flames for a long time, until my eyes begin to smart, until the heat blazing forth makes me aware that it is cold in the room.

I draw my knees up, rest my head on my knees, my arms around my legs. I sit and think of absolutely nothing until, out of this terrifying emptiness, I feel a roar in my head. I no longer know if the roar comes from the stove or from inside my head, which has been changed into a smithy with thousands of hammers pounding.

I don't know how long I sat there. Finally, I got up and, shakily, went in the direction of the door. I went out the corridor, where I was immediately hit by extreme cold. Cold light weakly illuminated the corridor. Holding onto the walls, I dragged one foot after another. I stopped in front of the *Ambulanz* door.

A ray of light shone through the keyhole, and I could hear muted conversation through the door. I could not make out the words, nor did I care to, but I heard the voice clearly, the voice that I could have recognized from among thousands of others. It did not matter what she said, the important thing was it was her speaking. Slawka! She was not asleep yet, she was there and somebody else was with her.

As quiet as a mouse, I passed the door and went on to the end of the corridor. I pressed my forehead against the cold glass pane of the door.

In the night, the clear beaten snow looked light navy-blue, glittering with millions of sparks, as if reflecting the spreading sky above with its multitudes of stars. I opened the door and was captivated by the majestic beauty of the night. I tried to catch the perfectly shaped stars of the snowflakes on the sleeves of my bathrobe. But not one of them wanted to last. They melted quickly, changing into bright drops of water, disappearing and soaking my sleeves. I went back, closing the door behind me.

I walked, shaking with cold. All was quiet in the *Ambulanz*, but the light was still on. Maybe it is Slawka? Whatever, I can always come in and ask for a sleeping pill.

I knock and enter. I am enveloped with warmth and welcoming light. Slawka stands near her desk. Perelka[25] is writing. What a beautiful, warm ambiance! Slawka! An unexplainable force emanates from her, hypnotizing me. At the sight of her, at the sound of her voice, I feel that I am losing control over myself.

*Ah, Hanka, come in, come in!* she welcomes me warmly.

*I am sorry to disturb you,* I mutter, *I just came in for a sleeping pill.*

*No, no come in, sit with us!*

Perelka got up and, exchanging a few words with Slawka, excused herself and left. We brought our chairs closer to the stove and sat down.

*You knew Jakub was there today,* Slawka opens the conversation. *He wants very much to see you and was very upset that I did not bring you along.*

*Never mind,* I answered, *Marta told me that they will be let go very soon.*

After a short silence, Slawka started to talk about my favourite topic, medicine. The silence of the night was disturbed only by Slawka's voice, talking about the new progress in fighting cancer and other terminal diseases. Late at night, we separated and went to sleep.

## The Executions[26]

*Kapo* Jakub tried his best to help the girls as much as he could. He apparently was ordered by the camp authorities to hang the girls, but refused. He tried to delay it by claiming that he had to have orders from Berlin to execute anybody. Perhaps he thought that, if he delayed long enough, the Russians would arrive first. Jakub wanted very much for me to visit Estusia. Such a visit was possible, since every day special cases from the *Revier* were allowed to go to the men's camp's main hospital for X-rays and special treatment.[27] Marta tried to bribe our chief doctor, Dr. Tetmaier, and Dr. Slawka to let me go, but it never happened.

The orders from Berlin came to execute the girls. Shortly before the execution, Jakub brought Marta a note that he had smuggled from Estusia. It said: *I know what is in store for me, but I go readily to the gallows. I only ask that you take care of my sister Hanka, so that I may die easier.*

Jakub brought Marta's response to Estusia: *Estusia, I promise that I will never abandon Hanka.*

---

25  Slawka's assistant, a Belgian Jew.

26  This section consists of a memoir written in Ottawa in March 1993.

27  This was an actual hospital for inmates, non-Jews, and, I imagine, occasionally SS men.

Marta (left) and Anna in Brussels, July 1945.

On January 5, 1945,[28] Marta came to take me out of the *Revier* to the camp. The whole camp was standing at *Appel*. Marta brought me to our *Block*, where Shari and Nellie[29] grabbed me. I wanted to run, to escape,

---

28 Gutman, Yisrael and Michael Berenbaum, eds. *Anatomy of the Auschwitz Death Camp* (Bloomington, IN: Indiana University Press, 1994) states the date of the execution as January 6, 1945. However, the correct date is January 5, 1945.

29 Two sisters from Slovakia who came with Marta into the camp in 1942. Shari and Nellie were well-educated, sophisticated girls who kept very much to themselves. I think that one of them was working in the camp *Sekretariat* (Administration) and one was the secretary of the *Block*. We knew them, but not intimately. There was usually little love lost between the Slovakian girls, who were the elite of the camp, and the rest of us. The relationship between Marta and us was an exception. Marta felt the animosity even forty-six years later in Israel, at the June 1991 dedication of the Yad Vashem memorial

but they held me fast. Suddenly, there was a thud of drums, a groan from thousands of throats, and the rest was mist.

The day after Estusia's execution, I got up to brush my teeth. I suddenly realized that the world would go on without her, that her death wouldn't make any difference to anybody. I lost my mind. I became a living corpse; I did not care if I lived or died. It was Marta who bodily took me out of Auschwitz during its final evacuation on January 18, 1945. It was Marta who dragged me all the way through the icy death march, through Ravensbrück to Neustadt-Glewe. It was Marta who fed me, washed me, cuddled me, and scolded me.

We were liberated by the Russians in Neustadt on May 2, 1945. The Russians turned us over to the Americans. The question was, *What do we do now?* I remembered the scorched ruins of the Warsaw ghetto. There was nobody there for me. And Marta? She wanted to return to Slovakia to look for her lost relatives.

I wrote my diary in Polish in June 1945, barely six months after Estusia's death. I was in the beautiful hills of the Ardennes in Belgium with my faithful, dear camp sister Marta and a group of Belgian survivors. We were all in a sort of summer rest camp, arranged through the generosity of the Belgian Jewish Community Organization.

Among them was also Roza Tabakman, thanks to whom both Marta and I were in Belgium. Roza and I worked at the same table at the Union munitions factory, where, when time and opportunity permitted, we talked,

---

to the four girls. She felt left out of the "Polish" gang. I couldn't persuade her to join us in the more informal social gatherings.

There was considerable animosity between Slovakian and non-Slovakian Jews. While this was a general feeling between the groups, there was certainly no animosity between us. A strong friendship, such as that among Marta, a Slovakian Jew, and Esther and me, who were Poles, was an exception.

Slovakian Jews were comparative "old-timers," part of the Auschwitz "establishment" (for instance, Marta's prisoner number is 1000). The Slovakian Jews helped the Nazis administer the camp, served as assistants to the SS, including as *Kapos* and *Blockältesters*. They had life and death responsibilities and were hated. I also believe that there was an ethnic animosity as well. They were responsible for rounding up other Jewish prisoners to work. An eighteen-year-old Slovakian girl was the *Kapo* of *Block* 25, the death block where the *musselmen* (Auschwitz inmate slang for prisoners who were in a state of hopelessness and apathy, physically and mentally weakened, and near death) were kept until they were gassed.

Marta felt animosity from the others because she was a Slovakian. All of the Union munitions plant survivors were Polish Jews. In any case, the animosity was so great it did indeed last for forty-six years. I believe that it will go on until everyone is dead.

mostly about food. Roza repeated over and over again that the best ice cream in the world came from Belgium. It had stuck in my mind.

Something stirred in me. Now was a perfect opportunity to taste the ice cream! I persuaded Marta that, while relatives can wait, ice cream cannot. Out of love for me, Marta came with me to Belgium.

Roza was right. We had ice cream, three times a day for a long, long time.

# The Ghost of the Past
# is Never Far Away[1]

In 1988, I had visitors from Belgium, Marta and her son Sami. Marta's express reason for the visit was to light a fire under me. She said that, while a lot had been written about the smuggling of the gunpowder at the Union munitions plant, the stories were incomplete and distorted. She said that they identified only Roza Robota's name, that they didn't identify the other girls who were executed or their roles in the plot.

At Marta's insistence, I joined a small group of survivors of the Union munitions plant in an effort to have a monument erected at Yad Vashem to honour the memory of the four heroines. I owe Marta my life. I had to obey her wishes. Rationally, I knew that she was right. Emotionally, though, I was angry and resentful about the past reaching forward to catch up with me.

Despite formidable bureaucratic obstacles, on June 19, 1991, in the Memorial Garden of the Yad Vashem Holocaust Memorial in Jerusalem, a monument was dedicated to the memory of the four girls – my sister Esther Wajcblum, Ala Gertner, Roza Robota, and Regina Safirztajn – who were executed by public hanging in Auschwitz on January 5, 1945, for their sabotage activities.

During the ceremony, my sister Sabina and I were given the honour of lighting the eternal flame. As we lit it, I suddenly saw both my parents, who were murdered in May 1943 in Majdanek, smiling at me.

As Sabina and I stepped back and the ceremony continued, Sabina bent toward me and whispered, *You know, our parents were here.*

I knew. After the ceremony I related the incident to my daughter, Noa. I wondered to her, *How is it that I did not see Estusia?*

*Don't you understand?* she said, *You couldn't see her because her spirit is alive.*

---

1  This section consists of a memoir written in Ottawa in 1993 and 1994.

In May 1993, I found myself on a trip back to Poland to see the death camps with a group of Canadian university students. They had expressed the wish to have a survivor of the death camps accompany them.

The day we went to Majdanek was a glorious spring day. The chestnut trees were in full bloom. The fruit orchards covered the earth with a pink canopy of blossoms. We drove past the checkered fields, green, sprouting wheat pushing through the rich brown earth.

From time to time, we could see farmers working their fields with horse-drawn ploughs. Flocks of birds would descend on the fields, picking up the seeds. We passed by families and farmers in their horse-drawn carts. It all looked so pastoral.

We arrive at Majdanek. I don't see the gruesome memorabilia in front of us. Instead, I am searching back in my memory, *Where were we? This block? That block? This camp? That camp?*

I respond when the students ask me questions, probing, sensitive questions, questions that bring back memories and associations that have been deeply buried. We come to the collective grave. It is a round mound of ashes that had been carefully scooped to rest in one place under a protective dome of gray stone. Somehow, the dome looks like a *kippa*[2] on the reassuring head of a father.

A student asks me, *How do you feel?*

I was glad that he asked me. If he hadn't, I would not have put my feelings into words. What I felt was relief. I had found my parents' grave. Finally, I can say a *b'racha*[3] over them.

When I answered the student, I felt that it wasn't me talking. I felt surrounded by thousands of faces, smiling at me, pushing me, yelling at me, talking to the students through me, *Tell them! Tell them! Thank them for us, for coming here, for remembering us and for never forgetting!*

Life goes on. Occasionally I am asked to speak as a witness, as a survivor, to give testimony to my experiences. I do it out of a sense of duty, a sense of obligation toward those that perished, toward those that want to know, for those who will not let the Holocaust be forgotten or denied.

But I do it reluctantly, fearfully, with many mixed emotions. I am afraid of not being believed. I fear the motives of my listeners. I feel guilty about having survived. I am afraid that people are not listening to what I have to say, but are instead overcome with emotion at seeing me. They become

---

2 Skullcap.

3 A prayer of blessing.

Reunion of Isabella (left) and Anna, 30 January 1994.

mute, not daring to ask me questions for fear of hurting me, who has been hurt so much already.

I don't know how to break through the wall of compassion between me and my listeners, between me and my family. So I continue to live, appreciating each and every day, with the ghost of my past hovering over and behind me.

It is never far away.

In January 1994, I received a package from my sister Saba. It contained a moving letter from Bavaria from a woman named Alexandra. The letter said that my nanny, Isabella, was very much alive. Isabella had been living with Alexandra's family since 1955. She had been nanny to Alexandra and her sister. There were pictures in the package. The pictures were of my mother with her classmates in 1905, pictures of my mother as a young woman, and pictures of Isabella.

I couldn't believe it. I ran to the telephone to try to contact Alexandra in Germany, but there was no listing for the family under the address. I grabbed a few pictures of my husband, daughters, and grandchildren and sent them off.

Not long after, I received a telephone call from Alexandra. I cried as Alexandra told me that for the last fifty-one years, since 1943, Isabella had never stopped believing that we girls had survived the war. She had never stopped looking for us. She had searched for us through the Red Cross, even through the "Rudi Carell" show, a television program in Germany specializing in the search for missing relatives. But it had been all in vain.

By coincidence, Alexandra had gotten into a conversation with an Israeli woman now living in Germany. The woman's mother is my sister Saba's neighbour in Stockholm, Sweden. Alexandra had immediately written to Saba, who forwarded her letter to me.

Alexandra told me that, though ninety-six years old, Isabella is in the best of health, her razor-sharp memory intact. I heard some noise in the background. Alexandra said that Isabella wanted to talk to me.

I could hardly make out Isabella's words, for they were the indistinct speech of the deaf, but I could make out "dear Anusia." I was thrown back to the time when I was five years old and felt Isabella's arms around me, loving me and hugging me. I decided then and there to go visit her.

Travel in or out of Canada during the winter can be an adventure. I had no problems travelling from Ottawa to Toronto, where I was to catch a connecting flight to Munich. I then waited two days trying to leave Toronto for Germany. Toronto's airport was closed for the first time in fifty years due to an unprecedentedly severe snow and freezing rain storm. But I finally got to Munich.

At the airport, I spot a statuesque blonde holding a card decorated with a big red leaf with my name written on it: Alexandra. Next to her, resplendent in fur coat and hat, is Isabella. I rush to embrace her.

The deaf-mute compensate for their lack of verbal communication through vivid facial expression. I can see in her face her first reactions of surprise, dismay, and wariness. Then as I hug her and look deeply into her eyes, I can see a sunny smile of recognition brightening her face. She bursts into a fury of sign language, which I no longer understand. Alexandra interprets – Isabella was expecting to see a twelve-year-old girl with curly black hair. In her memory, there had been no allowance for the passage of time.

Alexandra introduces me to her German husband Harro and to her mother Alina. Alexandra has also brought a friend to photograph the reunion. Alina hugs me as a long-lost friend. I immediately feel welcome in this warm and loving family.

They had travelled one hundred kilometres from their little town in Bavaria near the Austrian border to meet me. Alexandra tells me how worried they all were about the delay, how Isabella hadn't slept for two nights waiting for me to arrive. I listen to Alexandra, holding Isabella's hands all the way.

We arrive at the picturesque town. It is surrounded by the Alps. The scenery is breathtaking, the mountain air clear. The family occupies both sides of a duplex. Alexandra and her husband Harro live on one side of the duplex with their children, Alexandra's mother Alina, and Alina's sister Maria. On the other side live Alexandra's sister Ela, her German husband Siegfried, their three children, and Isabella.

The family treats me like visiting royalty. Food and drink are pressed on me continuously. I meet the whole family at dinner. After dinner, the men disappear and we women talk. Alexandra interprets Isabella's sign language for me. Slowly, her story emerges.

Isabella struggled through the war on her own, spending some time in a German labour camp. She eventually lived for a while with her brother in Wroclaw, but they didn't get along. In 1954, Isabella came to Falenice, Poland, to stay with her deaf-mute friend, Alexandra, who was the mother of Maria and Alina, and the grandmother of Alexandra and Ela. In 1978, the elder Alexandra left Poland and brought the whole family to Germany. She died in 1993.

Isabella brought up two generations of the family's children, and now, at ninety-six years of age, was helping with the third generation, Ela's children. Isabella loves them. Her face lights up whenever she talks of them. The children and the rest of the family adore her, too.

Ela and I laughed when I told her how I used to run to Isabella to escape my mother's wrath, how Isabella wiped away my tears. Ela said that Isabella did exactly the same for her.

Isabella told me how she had cried when she came to visit us in the *Wehrmacht* barracks in 1943 and found that we were gone. She knew what had happened. She knew that the Jews were transported out, but she firmly believed that the children would be spared and had never ceased to look for us.

Isabella asks me about my relatives, one by one. She remembers them all. On my father's side, my aunts, my uncles, my cousins, all gone, all murdered. With my eyes filling with tears, my heart constricted, we talk about how it used to be, how they used to be, how we used to be.

On the second day of my visit, Alexandra arranged for a newspaper reporter to interview Isabella and me. Harro asked me not to talk about the war. Because of the current nationalist sentiment in Germany and the demonstrations against foreigners, he was afraid of possible repercussions for the children at school.

By the third day, I had begun to understand Isabella's sign language, and Isabella and I could communicate on a more intimate level, without an interpreter. Alina and Maria also felt a little bit more at ease with me.

Isabella shared with me her longing for Warsaw and for the friends she had left behind. The old ladies, Alina, Maria, and Isabella, find themselves in a foreign land, in a foreign culture, isolated in a small village. Not knowing the language, they can't answer the telephone. All three of them miss and long for Poland, even though they all appreciate that they are well off where they are and feel lucky and happy to have their family around them.

The story came out in the newspaper about my reunion with Isabella. Even before we saw the newspaper, the children came home from school very excited. Their teachers had told them that there was a story about their family in the paper. It made them feel special and proud.

Even though I had not discussed the war, the reporter was perceptive and intelligent. She knew that I was Jewish and had been forcibly separated from Isabella. The article reflected her knowledge of the context. There was a lovely picture of Isabella and me, and in the side article the words, *The now ninety-six-year-old deaf and dumb woman was always convinced that somebody from this family had survived the Holocaust.*

Alexandra bought ten copies of the newspaper.

Proud of her command of the German language, she told me that she had understood every word of the article, every word but one.

She asked, *What does "Holocaust" mean?*

# Afterword

## by Joel Prager

Why another book on the concentration camps?

If the so-called revisionists or defilers of history have not been shamed and silenced by the previous outpouring of books detailing the moral depravity and predatory inhumanity that were the categorical imperatives of the Nazi concentration camps, why this book? What can the anguished memories of survivors do to bring about justice, to redeem the dead, when public memory fails? When the moral social contract and the ability to empathize have become progressively weaker over the years? When the call for justice and the thirst for revenge are frequently confused and assailed? Above all, when posthumous justice is at best a pinprick, fleeting as we turn the page and put down the book? The answer, as one might expect, is a complex one, and, in fairness, somewhat elusive.

Glibly, we can say, as did John Stuart Mill, that on great subjects there is always something to be said. In this case, we can say something is left to be rediscovered and remembered as part of our human heritage. This memoir contributes by making sure that the Nazis, despite their boasts and determination, will not "dictate the history of the *Lagers*" and allow their heinous crimes to be lost to memory.

The narrative, moreover, enables historians to fill in some of the gaps about who actually participated in the blowing up of one of the crematoria at Auschwitz, how the plan was hatched, how the gunpowder was obtained, how they were caught, and, of course, what happened to them.

It also provides documentary evidence of the intentionally designed dehumanization process developed and practised by the Nazis. The narrative fully documents how the dehumanization process operated, how camp inmates were violated and pummeled into submission until many lost their human dignity and, ultimately, the will to live.

These diaries, by necessity, are Anna's own story. It is a story that she herself has lived and witnessed, written from the vantage point of youth abruptly ended.

She begins by telling of her childhood, describing her parents, including their warts, her siblings and their rivalry, and the Jewish bourgeois world of Warsaw. This provides a context to help us understand her journey to the Nazi charnel house: how the world that she knew and felt secure in was suddenly wrenched from her. We also see the values that shaped her, how they were challenged *in extremis* by events she did not fully comprehend and that she was ill-prepared to grapple with, inasmuch as anyone could be well-prepared for Hell. Her privileged life and superior education were no defence against the deep darkness that awaited her and European Jewry, gypsies, Slavs, and those committed to the socialist or liberal-democratic tradition. Here we are able to celebrate and not scoff at and pity the camp's inmates.

The diaries are more than a record of events, they are a confession. They are Anna's way of seeking absolution for surviving. It is a desperate attempt to be free from an inexpressible grief that comes from the loss of a beloved sister, the sense of isolation, and the gnawing guilt for having survived.

Primo Levi captured this when he elegiacally wrote about his "shame of not being dead," of "what he had seen," "what others had done." With heartrending honesty he writes:

> We, the survivors, are not the true witnesses. We are an anonymous minority: we are those who by their prevarications, or their attributes or their good luck did not touch bottom. Those who did so, those who saw the Gorgon, have not returned to tell about it, or they returned mute.[1]

But Levi, despite his eloquence, is wrong. Like it or not, he is a witness; he has seen the Gorgon's head, and, as his many books testify, he refused to be mute. Anna, too, refuses to be mute, to let the ghosts of the past disappear. If there is absolution, even temporary absolution, it can only be gotten by Anna telling her story, reliving and expressing her torment, remembering and documenting the deeds of her sister and friends.

And, as readers, we can help by our understanding, empathy, and acceptance that those who died as well as those who survived did not do so in vain. Their scheme may have been hopeless, driven by desperation

---

1 Primo Levi, *The Drowned and the Saved* (New York: Simon and Schuster, 1988), pp. 82–84. There is also a discussion of Levi's struggle with having survived the concentration camp in Myriam Anissimov, *Primo Levi* (Woodstock, NY: Overlook Press, 1999), pp.162–63 and chap. 18.

and illusion, but their willingness to resist, not to passively accept the doom planned for them, inspires us precisely because of its expression of indomitability in the face of hopelessness.

On another, even more intimate level, Anna's narrative has three interconnected threads that make her story more than an accusation of the perfidy of the Nazis and a retelling of the fate of Jews in Auschwitz who, for some, were nothing more than another casualty of a World War that ultimately killed between fifty and sixty million people.

The first thread, as we have suggested, is that she has written her diaries because of the deep love she has for her sister, hanged by the SS for her part in the "gunpowder" plot to destroy the crematoria. In a world where love has become a commodity, surrounded by hype and hucksterism, it is easy to lose sight of its power to heal and to inspire. The sisters' love for each other protected them and gave them the will to go on.

The second thread is redemption. Anna felt responsible for her sister's becoming involved in the plot, and Estusia's death can only have meaning if we, the readers, discover who she was, what she did, and the price she paid for her actions.

To die for no purpose and to vanish in obscurity is something that Anna cannot accept and live with. While her sister has perished, Anna's memory of her has not, and in this way Anna has redeemed not only her sister, but herself as well.

Third, she is driven by the need for justice. But Anna's implicit demand for justice is not simply for her sister. It is for all of the camp inmates that were devoured by flames, destroyed by malnutrition and disease. Justice requires that they be treated as more than a statistic.

Finally, the publication of Anna's diaries represents a painful search for closure, the need to end her long nightmare that began more than fifty years ago. Her diaries are not simply a serious documentation of life in Auschwitz, or an exploration of the human heart, or a struggle to deal with large moral questions; they are an attempt to free herself from the ghosts of murdered inmates, especially her sister, and from "the experience of radical evil."

When Jews die, it is customary for family members and friends to put soil on the casket. The soil symbolizes the finality of life and the return to the soil. It is designed to give closure to the bereaved, to provide spiritual peace and permit the living to go on with their lives. As we know, there is no grave to toss soil on. But Anna's diaries are symbolically the tossing of the soil and a closing of the grave. It is therefore fitting that we end with the *Kaddish*, the Jewish Prayer for the Dead:

Magnified and sanctified be His great name in the world which he hath created according to his will. May he establish His Kingdom during your life and during your days and during the life of all the House of Israel, even speedily and at a near time, and say ye, Amen.

Let His great name be blessed for ever and to all eternity.

Blessed, praised and glorified, exalted, extolled and honoured, magnified and lauded be the name of the Holy One.

Blessed be He though He be high above all the blessing and hymns, praises and consolations, which are uttered in the world, and say ye, Amen.

May there be abundant peace from heaven, and life for us and for all Israel, and say ye, Amen.

*He who maketh peace in His high places may He make peace for us and for all Israel, and say ye, Amen.*

May you find the peace that you seek and deserve, Anna.
Amen.

# Index